When Parents Cry

JOY P. GAGE

ACCENT BOOKS
Denver, Colorado

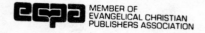

MEMBER OF
EVANGELICAL CHRISTIAN
PUBLISHERS ASSOCIATION

Second Printing, 1980

ACCENT BOOKS
A division of Accent-B/P Publications, Inc.
12100 W. Sixth Avenue
P.O. Box 15337
Denver, Colorado 80215

Library of Congress Catalog Card Number: 79-56358

ISBN 0-89636-045-8

for him
with whom
I cried
and
for our three
who also brought us
laughter

This is a book for parents . . .

Specifically, it is for parents who share a painful bond for it looks at the problems of youth rebellion. Lest the reader be betrayed, however, it should be understood that this is not a book on how to prevent rebellion. Nor does it offer an abundance of advice on dealing with rebellion in the home. It is a book written from the perspective of the parent who has tried everything but who is, nonetheless, faced with a casualty. It attempts to answer only one question: After the parent has done everything possible for his child, what can the parent do for himself?

CONTENTS

PART ONE
The Plight of the Parent

1   "Where Did We Go Wrong?"   *11*

PART TWO
Setting Standards for the
Wrong Reasons

2   The Care and Feeding of
     Disillusionment   *23*
3   Train a Child or Control a Life?   *33*

PART THREE
Revising Standards for the
Wrong Reasons

4   Politics, Peers and Parental
     Pressures   *49*
5   Perpetuating Parental Values
     in the Home   *61*

PART FOUR
The Parents Face a Casualty

6   Emergency Procedures for Coping
     With the Immediate Crisis   *73*
7   Eight Do's and Don'ts for
     the Post-Crisis Period   *85*

PART FIVE
The Parents' Right to Life

8   Is There Life After Johnny?   97
9   Can We Begin Again, Lord?   109
10 We Still Have Each Other   121

PART SIX
The Parents' Gift of Love

    "If" for Parents   135
11 Love Letters to Sons and
    Daughters   137
12 "The Greatest of These . . ."   147

    Postscript . . .   157

    Notes   159

PART ONE
The Plight of the Parent

1
"Where Did We Go Wrong?"

"Where did we go wrong?" "What can we do?" "Why did it happen to *us*?" "Why? Why? Why?" Such are the cries of parents everywhere who face the problems of estranged sons and daughters. It is a rare home which has not lost an offspring to the drug culture, the sexual revolution, the occult or pseudo-religious groups. Likewise, it is a rare parent whose initial reaction, when confronted with the problem, is not that of guilt and self-condemnation.

So much has been written about the child. So little

about the parent. Volumes have been produced in an attempt to analyze, defend, explain or correct this unencumbered generation with its unstructured lifestyle. Little has been said to encourage, help or comfort the parents in their heartache, disappointment and confusion.

Many have examined teens in an attempt to determine how their rebellion will affect the future of society in general. Few have thought it necessary to speculate on how those actions affect the parent. While conjecturing on the outcome of the collective younger generation, we have failed to see the implications of a generation of parents who are being debilitated by disillusionment, defeat and depression.

There are those, of course, who have written about the place of the parent in the total youth revolution. To blame or not to blame is usually the issue. But aside from placing blame or pronouncing absolution, little has been said from the perspective of the parent. The plight of the parent has been largely ignored. But the fact remains: when Johnny rebels, the parents—indeed the whole family—suffer.

With little regard for benumbed and bewildered parents, the unstructured generation has marched off in quest of something essentially its own, and in the process entire families have lost something which was corporately theirs.

Johnny rebels because he wants the right to live his own life, but in so doing he disrupts the lives of all others in the family. What he sees as a justifiable bid for his chosen lifestyle may constitute an irreversible blow to the family lifestyle. In altering his own future, Johnny may also permanently alter that of his parents and of his siblings. For them, time becomes a commodity measured by Johnny's actions. His act of rebellion becomes the dividing point between all their yesterdays and all their tomorrows. In their worst moments they pray that the latter will be mercifully few. Through it all, Johnny remains oblivious to the fact that in seizing his right to live he has thrust his family into an emotional limbo.

His is a generation of free spirits. They have been variously praised as the most promising generation and condemned as the ugly generation. By whatever name, their parents are troubled just the same. In a very real sense these parents have become the disillusioned generation.

Syndicated columnist Ann Landers once polled her readers as to whether or not they would choose to be parents if they had it to do over again. Out of 10,000 respondents, the answer was a resounding "no" from 7,000 parents.

In an article, "We'll Never Have Kids," published in *Woman's Day,* January 9, 1978, Marcia Kamien refers to the Landers report as a "large and perhaps not serious, negative vote" against parenthood. Ms. Kamien cited statistics to show that the number of couples opting for permanent non-parenthood is not alarming.

While Ms. Kamien presented some interesting ideas it should be noted that she was writing from the perspective of childless couples who were choosing to remain so. To use such opinions to diminish the importance of the Landers report is a false analysis of what Landers' readers were saying. Those readers were not childless couples who for reasons of convenience were choosing to remain so. Rather they were couples who had been there and back. Having balanced all the negative against all the positive, they had concluded that the heartaches outweighed the joys and that the experience of parenthood is altogether too traumatic to merit going through again.

It is not important whether their opinion does or does not influence childless couples to plan a family. What is important is that 7,000 parents have gone on record, saying, "We would never go through this again." When the nation's parents so adamantly voice their defeat and disillusionment, surely it is time they be heard. Surely it is a serious matter.

Specifically, I believe it is serious for three reasons. First, it is serious because so many homes are affected. For every parent who wrote in, how many were there who could not admit how they really felt?

Second, it is serious because of the variety of homes affected. As a committed Christian parent, I have been keenly aware of the number of my peers who are disillusioned over the rebellion of a son or daughter. I have also seen parents from other backgrounds who are crushed because a son or a daughter has opted for a lifestyle contrary to their own. Whether a conservative parent or a liberal parent, a Christian parent or a parent who has little time for spiritual things—with whatever philosophy one approaches parenthood, the parent hopes that his offspring will be a permanent part of the family life. When the child rebels and becomes estranged he leaves behind him parents who are, at the very least, bewildered, and at the worst, shattered.

Disillusionment is also serious because it is so emotionally debilitating to the average parent. In zombie fashion the parent moves through the daily routine. Whatever is accomplished in the way of work is accomplished through automatic reactions or not at all. The mental process is reduced to one thought. "I can't believe it. It's not happening. It can't be real."

One mother who had watched her daughter rush into a very bizarre marriage, then had to cope with the emotional effect of the marriage upon her daughter as well as the practical aspects of the divorce, expresses it thus: "Sometimes when I am thinking about my daughter or taking care of our grandchild I am overwhelmed by a feeling of disorientation (similar to loss of physical balance from an inner ear infection) that comes entirely as a surprise and I can scarcely believe that our daughter actually did it or that her baby is really real."

Sooner or later, depending on the personality and the circumstances, the parent will awaken from this state of disbelief and face the fact. It is real. It has happened. My world has fallen apart. It has come down around my ears and I haven't the vaguest idea how to put it back together again.

"It is so easy to slip into bitterness after the shock or grief has worn off," writes one mother. But bitterness is not very conducive to putting one's world back together again. The parent must begin to rebuild his life before bitterness makes a permanent inroad.

Rebuilding your life will not be accomplished overnight and even when it is done your world will not be the same as before. But it must be done. Putting your world back together again does not mean solving Johnny's problem or restoring the old relationship between Johnny and the family. It means solving the problems Johnny created for the family in the best way you can. It means finding a different relationship with Johnny. It means building a new family life for those who remain. It means making family plans which will not be contingent on Johnny's reactions or actions. It means picking up the pieces and getting on with the business of living.

In time, it will mean welcoming Johnny back into your world if he can respect it as your world. From the beginning, rebuilding your world must involve finding a workable relationship with Johnny. When the estranged off-spring is of age, the workable relationship will never be found unless the parents accept the fact that Johnny has the right to make his own mistakes.

This is a fact which many parents find hard to deal with. Before it is honestly faced there is apt to be a final hysterical scene in which the parents beg the child to reconsider his actions. The parent experiences an "I've got to do something" feeling which borders on panic. The resulting confrontation can be very ugly. There may be further attempts to engage friends or relatives, the minister or the doctor in an effort to abort the action. But there is very little a last-ditch stand can accomplish except to hasten the realization of the brutal truth. There is nothing you can do. At that moment it seems terribly frustrating to realize that your government can send a man to the moon and back but no one can tell you how to stop your child from destroying himself.

For the parent who has had some forewarning, the feeling of frustration may be magnified. Through a series of events, a parent realizes that his teen has set out on a course which is not only contrary to all the parent's values but is also clearly a self-destructive course for the child. Yet, for one reason or another, the parent is powerless to change Johnny's direction. No amount of counseling, coercing, or hysterics can stop the inevitable. The parent tries: "You should stay in school." "You should not be dating that girl." "Stay away from drugs." But it is no use. I think it must be rather like watching your child being consumed by a terminal illness.

Sylvia Vogel, a Jewish mother, relates her story concerning her daughter's decision to join the Moonies. The story reveals that, from the beginning, the mother was aware of the implications of her daughter's actions. Yet she was unable to stop them. On Mother's Day, Sylvia Vogel received word that the Moonies had picked her Jewish daughter and a black seminary student she hardly knew as one of 705 "perfect matches" for marriage.

This is Mrs. Vogel's story, quoted in part from the *Yuma Daily Sun,* May 16, 1979:

It was a "hammer on the head and a knife in the heart," said Mrs. Vogel of the engagement arranged by Korean evangelist and businessman Sun Myung Moon in a mass ceremony.

At her home in suburban Yonkers, Mrs. Vogel wept over the daughter she feels she has lost, a daughter she said "was emotionally bankrupt when the Moonies found her.

"She started having severe emotional problems when she was 13 years old. Her father had a massive coronary and was seriously ill for four years until he died. She became a loner."

(It was during the illness of her father that Ellen Vogel met a man who told her about a "one world crusade.")

Mrs. Vogel's story continues:

"He said he'd take her to one of their meetings," said Mrs. Vogel. "He never mentioned anything about a church, only the one world crusade."

After her daughter met the Moonies, Mrs. Vogel said, "She came home and said, 'They're all wonderful. They're young and happy and so beautiful.'

"I said, 'What about your religion? They never told you anything about this being a church.' "

Ellen was raised a conservative Jew with 10 years

of Hebrew schooling. She could read, write and speak Hebrew, and she has studied French, Russian, Japanese and Korean.

"Her brother is a rabbi," said her mother. "This is a girl who knew all the prayers. She didn't even have to open a book."

Two days after her father died in September 1973, Ellen moved out, telling her mother she was leaving to work with the church.

"When she left she told me, 'I'm Jewish and I'll always be Jewish,' " her mother said. But since then her mother said she has had little to do with the Jewish religion.

About all she can do for the present is "hope and pray" Mrs. Vogel said, adding there isn't a night she goes to bed that she doesn't "think about my baby."

Mrs. Vogel was one of those parents who had warning but could not stop the chain of events. For many parents there is no such warning. Suddenly one day when everything seems to be going right, the word comes. A telephone call from college: "I'm dropping out to join a commune." A discreet message from a friend: "Your son is living with his girlfriend." A surprise visit to your married daughter: she is sharing her bed with one man, her couch with another, and her husband is overseas. A call from your daughter-in-law: your twenty-one-year-old son has abandoned her for another woman. The juvenile authorities come: your sixteen-year-old has been picked up on drug charges.

Whatever the problem, however the parent learns of it, the discovery has to be among the greatest traumas of parenthood. It is as though, through a terrible accident, your child is wrenched away from you. In that moment you know that life can never again be quite the same.

One of the faults of human nature is that we are forever approaching our problems by analyzing them and establishing cause and effect. We get all involved in theories and statistics and forget about flesh-and-blood realities. "Who caused the mass youth rebellion?" we ask. And the theories pour in. The parents were too strict. No, they were too lenient. The children were over-indulged. Not true—they were neglected by parents who gave them everything but their time. The children had no spiritual guidance. To the contrary—religion was crammed down their throats.

From all the theories come a fresh set of statistics. The trouble is that, even if it were possible to correctly analyze the cause, in deciding who caused the great rebellion we do not diminish the pain inflicted by it. Theories and statistics meticulously charted are of little comfort to a parent whose offspring has suddenly become a statistic.

I believe it is time to look beyond the cause and deal with the effects. So this is not a book about what caused Johnny's rebellion or how it could have been prevented. Nor is it a book to tell you how to handle Johnny in the crisis of the rebellion. Hopefully it is a practical book for parents who are trying to find their way out of depression and disillusionment effected by Johnny's rebellion.

Three major areas have been considered: uncovering the causes of disillusionment (this involves parental problems with standards), coping with the casualty, and discovering life "after Johnny."

I am not sure if there is a foolproof formula to prevent rebellion. Neither do I attempt here to tell you how to correct it. But if you are a parent faced with this problem, I would hope in some way to encourage you to put the past with its devastating disappointments behind you. If you know someone who is faced with the problem, I would encourage you to show compassion. When parents hurt, it is a serious matter. It is imperative that they know someone cares.

Too often when parents cry, they cry alone. Some cry quietly. Some cry hysterically. Some cry behind closed doors. They cry for all their yesterdays. They cry because suddenly there are no more tomorrows. They cry for what might have been. They cry for what surely is to be. They cry out of anger. They cry out of frustration. They cry because they are afraid God does not hear them. And, I think, most of all they cry because they are desperately afraid that when parents cry, no one listens.

PART TWO
Setting Standards for the Wrong Reasons

2
The Care and Feeding of Disillusionment

Many writers who deal with the youth rebellion give considerable space to the question, "How do kids get that way?" Since I am more concerned about dealing with the effects of the rebellion than theorizing its causes, I would rather consider the question, "How do parents get that way?"

Why do parents react as they do to the problem of rebellion? How is it that parents can survive some of life's most devastating experiences and then be completely disillusioned by the actions of a son or daughter?

SETTING STANDARDS FOR THE WRONG REASONS

Parents predispose themselves to disillusionment

Disillusionment is sometimes born in the simple act of doing all the right things for all the wrong reasons. Parental disillusionment often stems from setting the right standards for the wrong reasons. It is one thing to set guidelines because one believes them to be right. It is quite another to set guidelines because one believes them to be the key to absolute prevention of rebellion.

The parent who fails to make this distinction sets himself up for disappointment. Assuming total responsibility for the outcome of parental training is unrealistic. Parents who set unrealistic goals concerning parental training are prime targets for disillusionment.

Case history: My disillusionment and how I acquired it

To say that I was disappointed the first time one of our daughters did something contrary to our values is to put it mildly. The fact that she was legally an adult and was on her own did not lessen my feelings of responsibility. My life fell apart. Coping was impossible until I faced the fact that I could not change what she was doing. Once I faced that fact it no longer made sense to ask, "Why is she doing this?" Admitting that I had no control over her actions, I began to concentrate on my own reactions.

I asked myself, "Why am I so devastated by what she is doing?" Only by frankly facing the past did I find the answers I sought. It didn't happen overnight but eventually I discovered that through my unrealistic attitude toward parental training I had set myself up for disappointment. That discovery was the beginning of my emotional healing. As a reader you cannot benefit from my solution unless you understand some of the factors which contributed to my problem.

I never expected the life of a parent to be trouble-free. I knew that along with the joys would come assorted heartaches. I expected to do some crying. I understood that in giving life to a tiny human being we would make ourselves vulnerable to a certain amount of pain. However, for the most part, I anticipated parenthood as a very wonderful experience. As we looked forward to the birth of our first child, it seemed as if time stood still. Yet my joy was mingled with sober reflections. For me, conception was singularly different from all of life's previous experiences. There was a pleasant finality about it which caused me to look at life a bit more seriously.

I believe that I was quite realistic about the negative aspects of childbearing. I recognized that, although the percentage is small, miscarriages, stillbirths and birth defects are all risks which accompany conception. The instant my firstborn arrived I asked the doctor, "How soon will you test her to see if she is completely normal?" Of course it was already apparent that she looked normal. But I wanted to make sure that she could see and hear. I never took the miracle of birth for granted. I gave thanks to God that our firstborn was normal. And our second. And our third.

My fourth pregnancy was abnormal from the beginning. So much so that only I knew I was pregnant. The doctor remained unconvinced. He scheduled my appointments at two-week intervals until we could agree on the diagnosis. When he finally came to a decision I was not prepared for it.

"You're pregnant," he said, "but you have only about a ten percent chance of carrying it. The fetus is not developing normally."

"Suppose I do carry it?" I blurted out. "Will the baby

be abnormal?''

His answer was evasive. "I don't think you will carry it," was all he would say.

In a rather confused state of mind I walked the few short blocks home. All I could think of was, "What if I do carry this baby and what if it's a boy and what if it's abnormal?" For some reason the thought of having an abnormal boy after three normal girls seemed the worst possible outcome of my condition.

As it turned out, the fetus (a boy) was not abnormal, but a fibroid tumor was complicating my pregnancy. The tumor, coupled with a severe case of the mumps, precipitated a miscarriage and ended my childbearing years.

Because I was aware of the implications from the beginning, experiencing a miscarriage was not as traumatic for me as it is for many other women. In the years to follow, I did have some fleeting moments when I longed for that incompletely formed little boy who left us before I ever held him in my arms. But for the most part I recognized that our loss was simply one of those risks which accompany conception, and I counted my blessings that out of four pregnancies we had gained three normal, healthy girls.

Somehow I was not so well prepared to face those other risks which accompany parenthood. I totally conditioned myself to believe that if I trained my children properly, the end result would be young adult offspring who would have the desire and the wisdom to make all the right choices. There would be no risk involved. I was sure that if I did everything exactly right my adult children would never disappoint me by doing what they knew to be wrong.

This is a very common misconception which is fed by numerous formulas proffered by well-meaning experts.

These experts infer that if you follow directions, your child will never rebel and his life will never fall apart. In effect they offer money-back guarantees. Certainly no one ever says, "There will be some casualties along the way."

The formulas for successful parenting vary from the highly permissive to the very strict. But no matter what approach one takes toward parenthood, the average parent chooses that approach because he believes he can control the end results.

The liberal parent sets out to eliminate the strict code of conduct in order that Johnny will have no reason to rebel. When Johnny finds a reason anyway, the parent is bewildered. The committed Christian parent teaches a strict code of conduct and tries to counter the influence of the world upon Johnny. When Johnny opts for a loose lifestyle, with everything the world has to offer, the parent is crushed.

Their approaches are vastly different, but these parents share one thing in common. Their reason for raising Johnny by a certain standard is to insure Johnny's continued living by that standard. The results are supposed to be predictable. But they aren't. The truth of the matter is that the parents' only responsibility is to train the child. However wisely, however conscientiously, however unselfishly the parents accept this responsibility, they must always remember there is no guarantee that Johnny will not rebel. Parents who assume differently set themselves up for needless heartache.

My sense of personal failure and frustration over my daughter's problem was overwhelming. The feeling was intensified by the fact that I had so conscientiously accepted my responsibilities as a mother. That meant reading all the books, avoiding mistakes I observed in others and praying daily for the children.

Because my husband is a minister I was in a unique position to observe parents from all walks of life. Our churches had parents whose children were a joy. But there were also parents whose hearts were broken by their children. Even as my heart ached for them I determined not to allow this to happen to me.

When our children were still very small we had a grand-motherly friend living nearby who was very fond of quoting the adage, "When children are little they walk on your feet. When they are big, they walk on your heart." I was not quite thirty and I had more answers than when I became forty-five. I saw very little need for a toddler to walk on mother's feet and I was certain that it was completely unnecessary for a grown child to walk on a mother's heart.

Although it seems ridiculous to me now, at that time I was convinced that I could make that old saying work in reverse. By teaching my children to respect my feet I thought that I could assure myself they would always respect my heart. Since my biggest aim in life was to be a good wife and a good mother, I assumed that my children would respond to my noble ambitions by never doing anything which would cause me undue pain or humiliation.

I know now that, while children are the source of life's brightest moments, a certain amount of pain is also inflicted by the parent-child relationship. It cannot be avoided. It comes with the territory. But as a mother of toddlers I was very idealistic and I went through each day with my blinders intact, involving myself in the all-important task of teaching my children not to walk on my feet.

I recall reading a magazine article at that stage of my

life which left me very unsettled because I recognized in it a warning signal which seemed to be aimed at me. The article indicated that it was sheer folly to allow the key to one's own happiness to be tied into the responses of another person. There was no question in my mind but that the writer of that article had people like me in mind. Certainly the thing which would give me the greatest happiness would be to see our children responding properly to their parental training. I wasn't just training them because it was my responsibility; I was training them because their response to that training was essential to my happiness. Had anyone suggested that their response might disappoint me, I would have said, "Then I'll try harder. I'll find a way." After all, there had never been a lack of magazine articles to help me find a better way.

This was the first article to imply that parental happiness should never be sought through a foolproof formula for successful child-rearing. Many people wrote about how parents could succeed at their job. Only one impertinent writer dared to suggest that it is a very foolish parent who depends on the outcome of his child-rearing efforts to bring about personal happiness. And only this writer, in some indefinable way, hinted that there was absolutely no relationship between protecting one's feet and protecting one's heart.

The article uncovered my blind spot. But in its place I built a defense. I knew that as Christian parents we had resources which the writer had not taken into consideration. My husband and I depended on the Lord for strength and on His Word for wisdom to raise our children properly. Surely the Lord would control the end result of that training. Nothing could have convinced me that I was heading blindly down the road to disappointment.

A dear friend of many years tells how she traveled a similar road. "It took me a long time to see that I had set myself up for heartache and disappointment," she confessed. "My children would all grow up to 'serve the Lord' as ministers, missionaries, or some kind of career service in related ministries. Hadn't we dedicated each one to the Lord privately and publicly? Didn't we have daily devotions, teach them to pray, encourage them to study their Bibles, take them to services, send them to camp, teach them right from wrong and keep them away from 'the world'?" When confronted with the problem of a rebellious teen she felt the confusion and disillusionment common to all such parents.

The story could be repeated again and again. Many conscientious Christian parents experience heartache because that sweet little child who once recited Bible verses on daddy's knee is now out there peddling drugs, selling flowers for the Moonies or sharing an apartment with a member of the opposite sex.

These disillusioned parents spend half of their time asking, "Have I failed God?" and the other half asking, "Has God failed me?" At no time does it occur to them to ask, "Is it Johnny who has failed?"

On the one hand the parent reasons, "If I am responsible for Johnny's training, I must have failed God." On the other hand he reasons, "If God is supposed to be controlling the end results, why didn't He prevent Johnny's rebellion?" In the confusion no one thinks to ask, "What is Johnny's responsibility here?"

Like my friends, when I was faced with a casualty I found myself in a maze of confusion from which there seemed to be no escape. After more than six weeks I was beginning to wish I had never left my mother's womb. Then one day when I least expected it I received some startling advice on the subject of parental responsibility.

During an informal after-dinner conversation, a visiting minister told those parents present that parents must expect some casualties along the way. After so many experts had tantalized us with formulas for success this man was telling us that there would be casualties along the way. After so many who said, "You were too strict," or "You were too lenient," this one said, "No matter how you try, there are going to be some casualties."

Our entire conversation that day was sparked by the questions of another mother who was present. Her children were rapidly approaching the teenage years. With the same speed she was approaching the panic years. All around her, she viewed teenagers from Christian homes making bad decisions, rejecting their training, turning away from God. Deacons, pastors, Sunday school teachers—hardly a home was left untouched by the problem of a rebellious youth. With increasing concern this mother was searching for that one vital key which everyone else had missed. If only someone could tell her how to raise her children in such a way that they would make all the right decisions! In essence she was searching for that formula which, if followed to the letter, would guarantee success.

Instead she was told there are no such formulas. Success is not guaranteed. Results are sometimes disappointing. "We must train our children because that is our responsibility," the visiting minister emphasized. "Just remember that as parents we are only accountable for how we train our children. They must account for what they do with that training."

Listening to his words I felt an unnecessary and extremely heavy weight of responsibility begin to slip away. My standards for child-rearing did not change. I didn't mentally revise my methods—only my motives. The disillusionment which had engulfed me did not instantly disappear, but that day there was a beginning. There was a light at the end of the very dark tunnel. I made a firm first step toward emotional recovery as I came to terms with the question of responsibility. Mine. My daughter's. God's. There would be more tears. Other problems with other daughters. But I would not again set myself up for disappointment through confused thinking over responsibility.

Not all parents have problems with a misplaced sense of responsibility. But all parents who seek recovery from disillusionment must begin with the same step. They must deal with the past.

Looking back is inevitable. It can only be valuable if it is done from the right perspective. So long as there are Johnnys who go astray there will be parents who ask, "Am I to blame?" and "Why is Johnny acting this way?" I looked at the past and asked all those questions. All I found was an overwhelming sense of failure, which is the common bond of all parents who cry. But then I dealt with the past by asking, "Did I set myself up for disappointment?" and "Why am I reacting this way?" Only then did I discover the underlying causes of my own disillusionment. Only then did emotional recovery begin.

3
Train a Child or Control a Life?

This chapter may not be for you. Not every parent sets himself or herself up for disappointment through faulty theology. But after I had begun work on this book something happened which convinced me of the need to include this chapter.

I read an article which stated that when young adult offspring of Christian parents rebel, it is the fault of the parent. The reasoning was based on Proverbs 22:6: "Train up a child in the way he should go: and when he is old, he will not depart from it." Some Christian parents and religious authority figures look upon the verse as a guarantee that a child, properly trained, will never rebel at any age.

The writer of the article concluded that the verse constitutes a promise to the parent. He further concluded that since God does not fail to keep His promises, it must follow that rebellion against childhood training can only result from parental failure. I realized then that no book of this nature would be complete unless the parent is given some answers for this rather cruel indictment.

That very day I sat down and read the Book of Proverbs through in one sitting. I underlined in red every verse which spoke directly of the responsibility of the youth. I underlined in blue every verse which spoke directly of the responsibility of the parent. By conservative estimate there are four times more verses which deal with the responsibility of the youth.

Taken in the context of the entire Book of Proverbs, 22:6 can hardly be interpreted as placing the total responsibility for adolescent rebellion upon the parent. The admonition to the parent is to train a child. The promise is that when he is old he will not depart from that training. The word doesn't mean mature and it doesn't mean older. It means old. But the problems of rebellion concern a third age bracket, the youth.

Are your problems being compounded by friends, peers, or religious authority figures who use Proverbs 22:6 to tell you, "It has to be your fault!"? Are you disillusioned because you have had to face the fact, "I can train my child but I cannot control his life from the cradle to the grave"? If so, this chapter is especially for you. Let's consider what the rest of the Book of Proverbs has to say.

The proverbs which deal with parental training and

rebellious youth may be divided loosely into five categories: (1) specific responsibility of the parent-teacher; (2) specific responsibility of the youth-learner; (3) the accountability of the youth; (4) the unmerited suffering of the parents of a rebel; (5) some specific ways in which to deal with a rebel.

Responsibilities of the parent-teacher

A parent is charged with the responsibility of disciplining the child. There are several reasons cited. First of all, the child needs discipline. If you fail to discipline a child in his early life, you will ruin him (19:18). A youngster's heart is full of rebellion, but punishment will drive it from him (22:15).

Certainly we have all seen young children who are completely undisciplined. They are out of control because parents will not put forth the time and effort required to discipline the child. These children have problems which are a direct result of parental failure. On the other hand, there are many well-disciplined children who grow up to rebel against parental values. We will see that later chapters bear this out. The parent should discipline the child because that is his responsibility. He is charged with controlling a child, not controlling an entire life.

The parent must also discipline his child in order to show his love for the child. In fact, if you refuse to discipline a child, it proves you do not love him (13:24). I have seen the truth of this principle attested to by youth who were going through a period of rebellion. One young woman told her family she wanted to live her own life in her own way without their interference. After several years she was still living her own life but she had completely reversed herself on the interference issue. She felt that a negative response from her family was better than none at all and told them so. She had found that, when her parents determined to withdraw their guidance (she was of legal age), their lack of input made her unsure of their love. Their discipline while she was growing up was recognized as an indication of their love.

The responsibility of the parent-teacher must, of necessity, include physical punishment. Sometimes mere words are not enough. Scolding and spanking a child help him learn (29:15).

Carl was the principal of a small rural school when we met him. He stayed in that school for sixteen years because he wanted his children to go to a school where they would receive discipline which would underscore the discipline they received at home. In discussing the problems of discipline, Carl related to us an incident which took place while he was attending summer school at a large western university.

The guest lecturer for the summer English course was a well-known writer. This lecturer made a statement to the effect that good teachers never need to use discipline. If the teacher makes the class interesting the discipline will take care of itself. Carl challenged this statement. (Carl had been teaching all those years while the guest lecturer was turning out bestsellers.) The lecturer promptly invited Carl to see for himself.

"I teach a class every morning," he said. "It is made up of the children of professors at this university. Why don't you sit in on it?"

Carl went to the class the next day. He found a seat in the back of the room from which to observe the teacher and the pupils. The lecturer was halfway through a very interesting period when two boys in the back of the room began to scuffle. The lecturer tried to ignore them. Then he tried to reason with them. Things got worse instead of better. The exasperated lecturer finally marched to the back of the room and physically restrained the boys. End of scuffle. End of demonstration. Carl left the room. Sometimes mere words are not enough!

The parent is admonished to use punishment that hurts because it drives evil from the heart and keeps the child out of hell (23:13,14). This passage also declares that parents should not fail to correct children because discipline won't hurt and they won't die if you use a stick on them. Certainly these passages cannot be construed to mean a blanket approval of cruel physical punishment, some of which does hurt too much and from which too many children do die. Obviously these children are the victims of sick or deluded parents and the Scriptures cannot be used to condone such actions.

A parent who cannot control his anger while disciplining a child should never use physical punishment. But a normal and rational approach to discipline sometimes calls for a bit of pain inflicted to the child's well-padded seat of learning.

Responsibility of the youth-learner

It is to the youth that the bulk of Proverbs is directed. An enormous amount of responsibility is placed on them for their behavior.

The initial subject of the book is the value of wisdom. The admonition concerning acquiring wisdom is primarily directed to young men. The first step in becoming wise is to trust and reverence the Lord (1:7). The theme is later repeated as we see that reverence and fear of God are basic to all wisdom and that knowing God results in every other kind of wisdom (9:10). It is significant that the key

to obtaining this wisdom is not found in parental training. Rather it is found in the individual's desire for
wisdom (2:1-5). We must assume then that while a parent
can discipline a child, he cannot make him wise. The
Lord is the only one who can give wisdom. Essentially
King Solomon is saying here that wisdom begins with a
reverence for and a trust in the Lord, plus a desire of the
heart to be wise. God responds to that desire by giving
wisdom.

The fact that wisdom is essential to well-being is spelled
out in 1:20-30. Those who spurn wisdom are given a
special warning: someday when you need wisdom because
you are in trouble, it will be too late. There will be no help
for your anguish and distress because you chose to ignore
all the facts; you refused to reverence and trust the Lord
and you lack the wisdom you need. This person must suffer the consequences of having his own way.

The most significant fact about this initial discourse is
that the responsibility is clearly and specifically placed on
the learner. Only fools refuse to be taught (1:7), and sons
are admonished to listen to their parents (1:8). We must
assume that however good the training, there will be some
who stubbornly refuse to listen. But those who do listen
will learn and will gain many honors. Chapter 23:22
repeats this theme as young men are admonished to listen
to their father's advice and to despise not an old mother's
experience. I like to think that this even gives me scriptural license to say, "Now when I was your age . . . ."

Not only are the young admonished to listen to their
parents; they are also told to assume responsibility for important areas of their life. They are to take care to stay
away from bad company, to refuse to emulate the actions
of the wicked, and to guard their affections. In fact, they
are to choose to follow the advice of their parents instead

of the suggestions of the wrong kind of friends (1:1-15). The youth are to assume responsibility for turning their backs on young toughs who rob, steal and kill. They are to stay away from people with whom crime has become a way of life.

What does this really say to us concerning the responsibility of the parent and the responsibility of the youth? Certainly as parents we are to teach our children all of these principles. But let it be noted that the principles are not given to parents as a training pattern. These principles are given to youth as a living pattern. It is to the youth that these proverbs are addressed.

There is a practical reason why youth must assume responsibility for their actions. Unlike children, youth are often away from the home without parental supervision. Once a child is old enough to attend school, community or church functions without parental chaperoning, the parent cannot be 100 percent sure what the child is doing every minute. The youth are admonished to make the right choices, as they have been taught to do.

Proverbs, chapter four, deals at length with avoiding the ways of the wicked. The youth are told to avoid the haunts of the wicked—to find their company elsewhere. An evangelist friend who is a former heroin addict relates how his entire life of crime began when, as a young boy, he began frequenting one of the city's biggest hangouts for gamblers and addicts. He knew it was wrong but he did it anyway. Today one of his chief messages to the youth is that a man is known by the company he keeps (Proverbs 13:20) and that he is also greatly influenced by that company. The biblical principle to avoid wicked company is a solid principle.

Guarding one's affection is important because the affections influence everything else in life (4:23). While we as parents must teach our children this principle, we may also have to face the fact that our sons and daughters may make some wrong choices in this area. Affections can be controlled. But they can only be controlled by the individual. As parents we can train and we can pray but the ultimate decision will be made by that son or daughter. In many cases when a daughter becomes out of control, a wrong choice is the root of the problem.

Recently a man confided in us that this was true in his home. The daughter first chose the wrong object for her affections, then lost respect for parental authority (they objected to her young man) and subsequently lost respect for all authority. The responsibility for her actions is clearly her own. In a related area, Proverbs deals specifically with sexual promiscuity by admonishing young men to stay away from prostitutes (chapters 5 and 7).

"Stay away from drink" is another admonition to the young. In a rather vivid account of the effects of alcohol the young man is told about the life of a drunkard. This passage (23:29-35) is particularly explicit in the Living Bible. The young are told about the hallucinations and delirium tremens as well as the silly things they are apt to say while intoxicated.

Through exposure to a close relative who was an alcoholic, my husband learned firsthand of its accompanying miseries. He was still a young man at the time and he determined then that if he never took the first drink he would never have the problem.

We have found the subject of liquor to be a sensitive one in many circles. Some churches have never deemed it as an evil to be avoided. Some which have traditionally avoided it are now taking the soft approach. Some believe Old Testament wine was not fermented. Others are sure it was. European Christians often partake of minimal amounts of wine with their meals.

Once in a small Italian town, my husband and I and our two daughters dined at a little country inn with a local pastor and his wife. As the host, the pastor asked if we would care for wine with our meal. My husband politely refused and our interpreter friend explained to our host that many evangelicals in America are total abstainers. Through the interpreter my husband then explained why he, personally, is a total abstainer.

The purpose here is not to discuss the final decision on the right and wrong of alcoholic beverages. The purpose is to show that this is one of many areas over which parents cannot exercise complete control.

There are many parents who serve liquor to their minor children. On a transatlantic flight I observed a couple with their fifteen-year-old daughter being served by the stewardess. When offered champagne, the mother refused, the father accepted and asked for one for the daughter. The stewardess refused to serve her. The father protested, "She is allowed to drink at home." But the stewardess was firm and tried to explain it was a legal matter. The matter was settled to everyone's satisfaction when the mother decided that she, after all, would have a glass of champagne. After being served, she promptly went to sleep without touching her glass. The father and the daughter drank the champagne.

It is unfortunate that some parents of this persuasion also serve liquor to the friends of their minor children. The serving of liquor to minors at teenage parties has become a great problem in many communities. Parents who conscientiously try to screen all the activities of their teens are sometimes quite unaware of the fact that liquor is so available to minors. Even for those who are aware of the problem, it is very difficult to deal with because the source of the liquor is usually a well-kept secret.

When our daughters were still in school, we knew that somewhere among the parents of their peers liquor was being made available to minors. But we had not one clue as to which home was involved. It was not until they had been out of school for several years that we learned the source. The information came quite by accident and, typically, it was the very last home we would have suspected. We never had reason to believe that our girls were using alcohol but we lived with the knowledge that it was available and that they alone could control their actions in the matter. It is highly significant that the warning about liquor is given to the young. Parents cannot control the youth 100 percent of the time.

The accountability of the youth

The fact that the responsibility for actions is put upon the young is further delineated in passages which speak of strong judgment on the rebellious young. God puts out the light of the man who curses his father or mother (20:20), and in the same vein (30:17), declares that a man who mocks his father and despises his mother shall have his eye plucked out by ravens and eaten by vultures. This may be seen to intimate an untimely death and reminds us that the first commandment with promise is to honor one's parents that one's days may be long upon the earth.

The unmerited suffering of the parents of the rebel

Further indication that more responsibility is put on the child-learner than on the parent-teacher is seen in two similar passages, 27:11 and 23:15,16. Here the father speaks to the son declaring how happy he will be *if* his son turns out to be a sensible man. The son who becomes a man of good sense is a public honor to the father. The father of a godly man has cause for joy. The wise son is a source of pleasure and the son is admonished to give his parents joy. There can be no doubt that the unmerited suffering which the parent of a rebel endures is said to be the fault of the rebel, not of the parental training. The father of a level-headed son is happy but the mother of a rebel is very sad (10:1, 15:20). The rebel is described as proud beyond description, arrogant, disdainful and one who feels himself to be faultless despite his many sins and despite the fact that he curses his mother and father (30:11,12).

Dealing with the rebel

Some specific observations about the rebel concern his lack of ambition, his unwillingness to be corrected and his negative effect upon his family. Perhaps one of the most sobering thoughts concerning the rebel is found in 11:29 which states that a fool who provokes his family to anger and resentment will finally have nothing worthwhile left.

In dealing with the rebel we are told what not to do. Don't try to honor a rebel. To honor a rebel is like tying a stone to a slingshot; it will backfire (26:8). How often we have seen people who would cure rebellion in this manner! But just as the verse states, the plan to cure by honor only backfires. Don't expect talking to cure the rebel. Talking to a rebel is sometimes useless. He will surely misapply an illustration and fail to get the point (26:9). Don't argue with the rebel. That only makes one as foolish as the rebel.

It is true that Proverbs 22:6 tells us to train up a child in the way he should go and when he is old he will not depart from it. Verse 29:17 also promises that if you discipline your son he will give you happiness and peace of mind. But these verses must be balanced with 30:11 which states that there are those who curse their father and mother, and with 12:1 which declares, to learn one must want to be taught. The same book which tells parents to train a child also tells parents not to waste time on a rebel or money on one who does not want to learn (17:16). In fact it must be borne in mind that if you would be rid of tension, fighting and quarrels, you must throw the mocker out (Proverbs 22:10).

To come to that point does not mean that the parent has necessarily failed. People who blame parents for the rebellious actions of a twenty-year-old are assuming that parental training means parental control, even over offspring who are legally of age.

Proverbs clearly holds the parent responsible for the training of children. Just as clearly, the book holds the youth responsible for many of his actions. If we are to discuss the theological implications of rebellion, then we must examine more than one isolated verse. We must balance Scripture with Scripture. It is theologically inconsistent to say that Proverbs 22:6 guarantees that a child will never rebel so long as he has received proper parental training. To apply this verse so universally and without regard to circumstances is to render the rest of the Book of Proverbs meaningless.

PARENTAL PROJECT
Setting Standards

Project: Working weekend for parents
Get away if possible.
Take along plenty of paper, pencils (include a
red one) and a cooperative spirit.
Set aside a definite time to work. Plan to follow the working period with a walk, a
swim, dinner out, etc.

Discussion Time #1

Begin by discussing the value of standards to you
and to your child. Try to isolate why you and your
mate feel you should have any standards. (If you find
that your goal is to control your child's behavior pattern for life, better reread chapter two.) Try to determine how extensive your standards should be. For example, one theory on standards is, "We don't make
many rules, but the ones we make are to be obeyed."
Whether you agree with this or not, try to state your
theory as clearly.

Work Time #1

Working separately, list what you consider to be
proper standards. Then compare lists *without comment.* Proceed to formulate a common standard in this
manner:
1. Underline in red all those items which both of
    you listed.
2. Place a red check beside those which are only on

your list but with which your mate essentially agrees.

3. Place a red question mark beside all others.

Discussion Time #2

Begin with statements with red checks. Discuss them one by one until you have covered statements on both lists. Does your mate feel a statement should be modified? More clearly defined? When you have agreed on the final form of all checked statements, you are ready to tackle those statements marked with a red question mark. But you may wish to take a break before you do.

Discussion Time #3

These may be harder to manage. Keep the tone of your discussion civil. Let the one who proposed the statement explain *all* the reasons behind it. Final decision on the statement should be made on one of three levels:

1. You're absolutely right. I just didn't think of it.
2. I don't feel as strongly about it, but I believe you are right.
3. I don't agree with you all the way but I'll stand with you all the way.

If an impasse is reached—one of the above cannot be used and the parent who proposed the statement is not convinced it should be dropped—go on to the next statement. Take some time to think. Come back to it. Remember, the object of the project is to find a standard upon which you will be mutually agreed.

PART THREE
Revising Standards for the Wrong Reasons

4
Politics, Peers and Parental Pressures

The standards which parents set are constantly questioned by the experts, by the neighbors, by the children, and even by the parents themselves. Parents should not depend on support of their standards as a verification of the need for demanding them. Someone will always be around to challenge what the parent is trying to do. It is easy to lose perspective under a barrage of criticism, and parents become so confused that they tend to revise their standards for the wrong reasons. They begin to wonder, "Do I have the right to demand this of my child?" or,

"Should I make some drastic revisions in my standards?"

Revising standards for the wrong reasons

One friend asked, "Should we insist that our youth cling to our old morals or should we roll with the punches? And if we roll, how far shall we roll?" A parent in this quandary should ask himself, "Why am I considering rolling with the punches?" (or "Why am I adamantly refusing to do so?"), "Am I giving in simply because I think it will give my child less *reason* to rebel?" (or, "Am I refusing to budge because I think it will give him less *room* to rebel?"). In other words, is the decision being made in order to find a way to control Johnny better or to control him for a longer period of time?

When parents begin to question their own standards it is usually because they are looking at those standards from Johnny's perspective. They begin to wonder how Johnny will react. I would advise parents in this position to move very cautiously. Don't change standards which you believe to be right in the hope of assuring control over Johnny. You may be disappointed.

Certainly I do not advocate rigidity. But a parent does have the right to set standards which he believes to be right whether or not Johnny accepts those standards. To begin reversing, lowering, or changing those standards in an effort to control the child will usually result in only one thing: while attempting to maintain control over the child's life, the parent loses control of his own. If this happens and Johnny still rebels, what does the parent have left?

Admittedly, setting standards can be a problem. But it should not become more complicated because the parent is looking at it from Johnny's perspective rather than his own. A parent has the right to set standards with which he is comfortable. So long as he is responsible for Johnny, he has the right to demand certain things of Johnny.

Biblically based standards questioned

Our own standard of child-rearing was as biblically based as we could make it. I strongly advocate this for every parent. We can expect any biblical principles which deal with human relationships to be good sound principles. After all, who knows more about human nature than the God who made us?

We arrived at our standard out of personal conviction, not out of necessity because my husband is a minister and, therefore, had to maintain a certain image. We never had a double standard (one for home and one for the congregation to see). In fact, we let our girls know that our standards had nothing to do with the fact that their father was a minister. We would have had the same standards no matter what profession he followed.

As a mother, I also endeavored to have an understanding with our congregations. I have never objected to other adults correcting my children. (I have, on occasion, corrected children other than my own.) However, my one request was that it never be done on the basis of, "You are the minister's daughter; you ought to know better." Rather, I preferred that they simply say, "You should not do that," or "You're old enough to know better." To my knowledge, no one in our congregations ever disappointed me in that respect.

Of course I am aware that Christian standards have been under a lot of scrutiny during the past decade because of the moral pressures of our age. Questions have been raised repeatedly. Can biblical principles provide a basis for meeting the pressures and problems of the twentieth century? Can the younger generation relate to Christian principles? Can our churches meet the continuing needs of today's youth?

Under the pressure of these issues we have seen teens rebel, parents panic and churches flounder. We have also noticed that solutions multiply. Making faith work becomes the name of the game and everyone wants to write the rules. The theologian declares it's time to change the message; the innovative youth pastor says it's the methods which should be changed; and the Sunday school curriculum editor insists that it is once again time to revise the revisions!

Then there are those who want nothing revised or changed. But change is all around. Traditional worship services are replaced by new formats, music takes on a new sound, and nearly everyone has a new look. People emulate fashions, throw away razors, give up trips to the barber and adopt new vernaculars, all in the attempt to make Christian principles more acceptable. I will concur that some change is necessary but when these changes are made in an attempt to make Johnny more comfortable with Christian principles, the perspective is soon lost.

No one can deny that parents today face some very complicated problems in the area of moral standards. Last night's telecast, today's newspaper, this week's news magazine—all bring details of current confusion:

The courts and the medical profession are again trying to decide what is right or wrong with abortion, infanticide and genocide.

Advances in the world of medicine have created a terrifying limbo in which man may be kept alive but not made well. The old are forbidden to die and the unborn refused the right to live.

Man and woman have long since won their right to live together *without* a marriage license. Now the news media reports that man and man are demanding the right to live together *with* a proper marriage license.

The reminders of the moral pressures of the twentieth century are always with us. Our sensitivity is shocked and it is natural to assume that the moral confusion is so great today that parents should revise the standards to accommodate peer pressures on their teenagers.

To those who feel that Christian standards are unrealistic, may I point out this fact. If world conditions ever constituted a legitimate excuse to give up our personal standards, Christianity would have died in its first generation. The problem of Christian living in a non-Christian world is as old as Christianity itself.

Christianity was born into a sick and dying society. Witches, pornography, obscene theater, violent entertainment, prostitution, formal contracts between homosexuals—such was the insanity of the world into which Christianity was introduced. Divorce was granted to either party with almost no contest. Men curled their hair and their long flowing beards. According to Will Durant, it was an age which produced men of intellect without morals, abilities without scruples, and courage without honor.[1]

As a Christian mother, I do not believe God is taken by surprise. I believe He made full provision for every pressure of every generation. He laid down the principles for handling the "new" morality on its first time around nearly 2,000 years ago when it was known as Roman immorality.

Through the Apostle Paul, God told the early Christians to separate themselves from the standards (or lack of them) in the world around them.[2] Constantly these early believers were challenged to a higher moral standard. God never said it would be easy. He simply said this is the way a believer should live. Since that time every generation has had to face its own set of moral problems and pressures.

Withstanding pressures

Whether or not the standards you have set for your home are biblically based, I believe this rule applies: if you have set a standard which you believe to be correct, don't revise it because the moral pressures of the age are so great. If parents look for easy solutions, it is not likely that they will be able to set any personal standards for the home.

Lest anyone think that I am advocating that parents completely ignore their teenager's feelings about standards, let me state what I believe to be an important principle. A parent should develop the ability to listen sympathetically without condoning a questionable action. It is one thing to deal with Johnny's problem in accordance with your standards. It is quite another to hysterically tell Johnny that he shouldn't have the problem. Obviously he does have it. The parent should listen, but there will be times when the parent must close the conversation with a firm but sympathetic conclusion: "I may be wrong but so long as I am responsible for you, that will be my decision."

Recently I overheard a mother of our community commenting on an incident which took place while her son was in high school. It seems that he had been cautioned not to take the family car to a certain place because the road was torn up and would likely be very rough on the tires. Not only did he take the car anyway, but he completely ruined a tire in the process. His mother told him he would forfeit the use of the car until such time as he had earned enough money to pay for the tire which she had replaced.

"But Mom," he wailed, "I have a date tonight."

"Then you had better go in the house and call her and explain that you have no car tonight," she told her son.

I admired her objectivity, but the point which really interested me was what she said next. A neighbor man was on the scene and heard it all. When the son was out of earshot he said, "You're awfully hard on him. For two cents I'd give him the keys to my Cadillac for tonight."

The mother told her neighbor that if he ever did such a thing he would have her to contend with, and that so long as she was responsible for her son, she would discipline him as she saw fit.

This incident reminded me of another problem parents face in maintaining personal standards for the home— that of constant interference from outside the home. Neighbors, relatives, schools and legal agencies are all guilty of criticizing the parents for standards imposed on the children. I think this mother did a wise thing when she let the neighbor know how she felt. Too many times a parent allows this type of pressure to confuse the issue at hand.

Sometimes the outside pressure takes a more subtle form. I recall one period of time in which one of our teenage daughters developed a close friendship with another girl whose parents held standards similar to ours. Before long I noticed that when my daughter asked if she and

Cindy could do something together, she always worded it the same way. "Cindy's mom said whatever you decided was okay. If I can go, she can go."

As time went along I got the same question, even when I was sure that Cindy's mom might not approve of what our daughters were planning. Finally I called her and asked her opinion of the latest plan.

"Oh, no," she said. "I don't want Cindy to do that. But I was sure you would say 'no' so I just told Cindy that whatever you decided would be okay."

I pointed out to her that, because she was avoiding her responsibility, my relationship was being severely strained with both girls. Fortunately, we were good friends and she immediately corrected her error. I never had to deal with that problem again.

Special problems concerning minors

Although we have never faced the problem of a minor out of control, I have seen many, many parents in our churches who have had to face this situation. Contrary to what some believe, I do not believe that the parents are usually to blame. I am overwhelmed at the complexity of the problems created by a minor out of control. I am appalled at the interference with which the parents must contend when they attempt to deal with their child. Some children have an uncanny way of convincing the neighbors, the juvenile courts and the school counselors that they are being misunderstood and mistreated, even when this is not the case. A subtle form of blackmail develops as soon as the child learns that there are those who will listen to him and that as yet his parents have not discovered where to tell their side of the story.

I would not for a minute question the fact that there

are abused and battered children in our country who are the helpless victims of sick parents. Nor would I deny that there are teenage girls who are sexually molested by their stepfathers or biological fathers. But we have seen the other side of the coin.

We have seen the sheer frustration of parents who know they have a child out of control and no one is listening. We have seen the thirteen-year-old girls who cry rape, accusing fathers, brothers, stepfathers and stepbrothers, when in fact it was not the case. We have seen thirteen-year-olds involve two sets of parents and the juvenile court in an endless argument over who should be in charge, simply by accusing one of the parents of cruelty. Of course in time the truth comes out and the parents are absolved. But in the meantime the parents live a nightmarish existence.

Strangely enough, their primary concern is never for their own reputation which surely is at stake. Their real concern is for their child who is definitely out of control but who is still managing to control the situation. These parents know that their child will, in the end, lose more than anyone.

One of the most frustrating cases we ever observed was that of a girl, age 15 (going on 30), who was keeping the entire family in a turmoil. She developed a very serious relationship with a nineteen-year-old young man who was out of school. Everything possible was done to keep the daughter from dating or seeing the young man. But, as is often the case, it was to no avail. Eventually the daughter told her mother that she wanted to marry the young man. Of course the parents refused. The daughter then threatened to go to the birth control clinic to get the pill. If they couldn't get married, at least they could sleep together.

After thinking it over, the mother decided that perhaps

a teenage marriage was the better solution. She relented and gave her consent. The crowning blow came when she discovered that while it was completely legal for her fifteen-year-old to be given the pill without parental consent, it was legally impossible for her to get married even with parental consent. In her state there is a minimum age law for marriage, but none for receiving contraceptives at the birth control clinic.

This morning I called the family planning center in our own city to check on local law. I was told that the pill is given at the discretion of the nurse in charge. Parental permission is not required. The nurse bases her decision on whether or not she feels the girl to be responsible. There is no minimum age requirement to receive this service. Perhaps it is time that conservative parents become more politically active in matters which concern minors.

It is difficult to be legally responsible for someone whom you cannot legally control. The responsible person should be allowed to control the decision.

While discussing this subject, one mother remarked that she had refused to allow her son to participate in a certain high school activity. She believed it to be too dangerous. "So long as I have to pay your doctor bills, I will have to forbid you to do that," she told her son.

While I might not have made the same decision, I agree 100 percent with her reasoning and her right to make the decision. It is a principle which we should endeavor to carry out at all levels, whether decisions are being challenged by our children, our peers, or our government agencies.

Factors which prevent satisfactory solutions

The times in which we live complicate the problems of

parenthood. But the root of the problem is not the moral pressures in themselves. As has been pointed out, every pressure this generation feels has been felt by some generation in the past. There are two factors which make our times different.

The first is the legal interference in the home. Someone outside the home dictates what is right for the child but assumes no responsibility for the child. The second is the prolonged period of adolescence in which a child demands all his rights but assumes no responsibility. Until something is done about these two factors, parents will continue to face some problems for which there are no satisfactory solutions.

Changing standards will not guarantee control over minors

I believe that parents are very concerned about this issue of control. A *Better Homes and Gardens* issue contains an enlightening article, "What's Happening to the American Family?"

The author polled parents on two questions. (1) At what age do parents lose control? (2) At what age should parents relinquish control? Amazingly, the answers showed that the majority of parents believe they are losing control long before they should. Sixty percent of the parents polled believe that control should be relinquished when the child is between the ages of 19-21. This would seem to indicate that many parents believe that parental control should be maintained until the child is of age. But in spite of what they believe is right, 54 percent of those same parents believe that teenagers are out of control today before they are 15. And of that number, 24 percent stated that the child is out of control before the age of

13.³

If you are a parent with a minor out of control, I would not attempt to give you some simplistic solution for your complicated problem. But I would encourage you to try to keep your perspective. If you have carefully thought out a standard for your home, don't change it because your child has learned to manipulate everyone around or because the local birth control clinic dispenses pills on demand. Remember that a standard is not set on the basis of whether or not everyone will adhere to it. It is set because it is right. If Johnny refuses to obey, don't change the standard; keep trying to change Johnny.

Finally, a word to those who may not have a personal relationship with Jesus Christ. I have a list of things in life which I would hate to go through without the Lord. Being a mother of teenagers tops the list. I could not have survived those years without Him. May I encourage you to put your faith and trust in Him. Even when you cannot satisfactorily control your child's life, you can find personal comfort if you will pray, "Lord, take control of my life."

5
Perpetuating Parental Values in the Home

In considering parental problems with standards, two general areas have been examined: setting standards for the wrong reasons and revising standards for the wrong reasons. In the latter category there is one final problem to be considered. It is that of relinquishing control of adult offspring.

The parent must recognize that as an adult Johnny has the right to develop standards which differ from that of his parents. But the parents should not revise the standards of the home to accommodate Johnny's chosen lifestyle.

Reflecting parental values in the lifestyle of the home

It is essential that the parent differentiate between controlling the lifestyle of the home and controlling the offspring for life. For example, Johnny takes an off-campus apartment at college and rooms with his girlfriend. He wants to continue his living arrangements during a weekend visit to the parent's home. He may even apply a great deal of pressure on his parents by using such logic as, "It would be hypocritical to have different rooms at home when we share the same bed every night."

The issue becomes very confused as parents and son are drawn into an argument over who has the right to determine the moral habits of an adult son. The parents declare, "We'll never approve" and Johnny counters with, "I'm of age." To settle the issue many parents find it necessary to send an SOS to Ann Landers or Dear Abby asking, "What shall we do?"

The real issue involved in the weekend visit question is not, "Who controls Johnny's morals?" Obviously he has already settled that question to his own satisfaction. The issue is, "Who controls the lifestyle of the home?" It is not a matter of the parents saying, "Johnny, we will not allow you to live this way." It is a matter of saying, "Johnny, we will not allow this in our home." It is the right of the parent to determine what goes on in the home.

In *Today's Health*, one writer expressed it thus: "Parents should make their reservations clear if they have them; i.e., if they do not condone sleeping together outside of marriage, then they must not allow this in their home."[1] Johnny may go through years of fighting against parental values. These years will be a time of great confusion and clouded issues if the parents fail to follow this principle.

The standards which determine the lifestyle of the home should reflect the values of the parents. From the beginning, parents will develop guidelines which reflect their values. This is not something which must be thought out. It is quite natural to train young toddlers out of the background of one's own set of values. It is only as the children grow up and those guidelines are challenged that it becomes necessary to define parental values more clearly.

It is not my purpose to tell you what those values should be. Instead I want to emphasize that whether being developed or being revised, guidelines should always reflect parental values.

Maintaining control of the lifestyle of the home

Controlling the lifestyle of the home is not the same as controlling the offspring for life. While the parents have a responsibility to control minor children, their chief responsibility toward adult offspring is to counsel. Parents cannot apply rules made for fifteen-year-olds to adult offspring. To do so only antagonizes and alienates these older children. But a parent may continue to control what goes on in his own home regardless of the age of the children. There is a vast difference in trying to tell Johnny how to live and in telling him what is permissible in the parental home.

There are many statements made in this book which concern adult offspring and would not be applicable to minor children. Certainly a twenty-one-year-old son who is tearing the family apart may be handled differently than a fifteen-year-old son who is doing the same. On the other hand, a twenty-one-year-old son who is living in harmony at home should expect to have more freedom than his fifteen-year-old brother.

It is amazing how parents easily lose this perspective. They find it very difficult to make a variation in the rules for separate age groups. And they completely fail to see that some rules are perpetuated regardless of the age group. Parents have the right to impose behavioral standards in their own home. These standards are not subject to vote or to veto by offspring who refuse to accept parental standards.

Distinct age groups versus family democracy

Parental perspective concerning age groups within the home is often clouded by outside forces. When our children were growing up, one of the popular issues was "togetherness." The age groups within the home were ignored. Even the distinction between parent and child was minimized. Supposedly this avoided fragmenting the family. Not only did the experts suggest that the family do everything together, they also strongly advised that children sit in on most of the decisions. Almost without realizing it many parents came to view the ideal family as a democratically run unit.

In theory it sounded good and I suspect that it sold a lot of magazines during those years. But in practice it didn't work. (Theories which portray children and adults functioning as equals seldom prove to be workable.)

Like other parents, I am sometimes subconsciously influenced by current trends. I found myself trying to apply some of those togetherness theories to the decision-making process in our home. It could hardly be described as a successful venture.

I recall attending a seminar for parents in which we were discussing family planning for family happenings. Somewhat frustrated, I asked the leader how one might go about discovering something the entire family would enjoy. I explained that I was conscious of the fleeting years and wanted to do things with my children which would count for the years ahead. Specifically I wanted to be able to go to bed at night knowing that, "Today we created a memory." But with everyone in on the planning session, nothing was getting done. What appealed to one child was boring with a capitol "B" to the others.

One woman whose children were grown responded to my question with a simple statement: "I do not remember ever asking my children if they wanted to go on a picnic," she said. "When my husband and I decided we had the time and the children had the need for a picnic, I simply packed a basket and we took them on a picnic."

Since that day I have made many additional discoveries which underscore her theory. A former classmate from high school days went with her husband and two young children on an extended cruise in their sailboat. Although they had not initially planned it that way, they eventually sailed from the Virgin Islands through the Panama Canal and home to the Port of San Diego. In describing the experience to the local press afterwards, Peggy laughingly remarked, "At no time were the children in favor of this cruise. Not at the beginning, not at the end, and at no time in the middle." But of course when it was over they were glad for the experience.

The point is, whether it is a simple picnic or an exciting round the world cruise, if it is purely a democratic decision, chances are that no memories will be made. Certainly there is a need for a creative means to train children in the decision-making process, but to strive for total democracy as a family is ludicrous.

Weaknesses of the democratic process would be a very minor problem if confined to such questions as what to do for family recreation. The topic would have very little to do with the subject matter of this book. But parents who think of the family as a democratic unit habitually try to handle problems by some type of democratic process. By the time Johnny reaches the prime age for rebellion the parents have become convinced that they do not have the right to impose their own values upon their children.

The democratic process should never be employed to determine or to control the lifestyle of the home. Such decisions are the responsibility of the parents. The minor child fits into the lifestyle primarily through the aid of rules which are laid down for him to obey. The adult offspring living at home fits into that lifestyle primarily out of respect for his parents.

From rules to respect

When our daughters were growing up they always had a curfew. In the beginning they knew only one thing about that curfew. They had to come home at a certain hour because their parents believed that they were too young to be out any later. It did not matter what time their friends went home. It did not matter that they did not agree with us about the curfew 100 percent of the time. Their curfew was determined by parental values. They obeyed the curfew because they were forced to and were punished if they failed to meet it.

However it was interesting to observe how they each continued to honor this curfew as they grew older. Each of them lived at home for a period of time after they were of age. Two of them lived at home throughout a lengthy engagement period. During the time of their adult years at home we made no conscious attempt to force them to keep a curfew. But each of them honored it. They either kept it, made prior arrangements over an anticipated late date or apologized when something unexpected detained them. They did not do this because they were too young to decide when to come in but out of respect for us.

Just prior to moving away, our youngest daughter discussed the curfew issue with a friend. The other girl was having quite a hassle with her parents over the late hours (early morning, to be exact) she was keeping. Because she was of age she felt her parents should not try to tell her how to live. But our daughter said to her, "I'm a year older than you and I still wouldn't think of keeping those kinds of hours. So long as you're living at home you have to remember that parents worry a lot and lose too much sleep if you stay out so late."

The elusive goal

The key to prevention of rebellion continues to be the most sought-after goal of millions of parents. It is, and will continue to be, an elusive goal. No one can tell you how to raise your child in such a way that you will never have to cope with the problems of rebellion. There are no success formulas. Only success stories.

Recently I discussed this topic with a young friend. She cited several middle-aged couples with whom she and her husband are intimately acquainted and whom they greatly admire. Currently these couples are facing problems with their teenagers. My friend is supportive of the parents and their child-rearing methods. She does not view their present crisis as an indication of parental failure. She believes the parents have done everything required of them. Yet their teens are rebelling against parental values. My friend has been deeply affected by the experience of these parents. As yet childless, she confided in me two reasons for remaining so. One is the nature of her husband's work and the other is the fact that neither she nor her husband feel emotionally prepared to risk the heartbreak which their friends are experiencing.

Through our conversation as well as through my own observation I noticed that my friend is criticized for her childless state by people who paint rosy pictures of the joys of parenthood. When she voiced her concern over this I encouraged her to remember it is a very private decision and should not be affected by pressures from insensitive outsiders. Then I reminded her that in life every situation has a set of joys and a set of heartaches. Certainly there are joys peculiar only to parenthood which she will never experience. On the other hand, there are some heartaches which definitely come with the territory. These she will escape. Only the idealist paints parenthood as all fun and games. Only the cynic declares it to be nothing but pain.

When children pass through the teenage years into young adulthood, parenthood becomes something which is characterized by confusion. Confusion over when to change parental standards is a perpetual problem. If a parent finds it necessary to revise his standards it should be because of personal conviction. Parents may find it very difficult to control a minor child. They may find it preferable to relinquish control of an adult offspring. But parents must never relinquish control of the lifestyle of the home. It is their home. It must reflect their values.

PARENTAL PROJECT
Revising Standards

Project: Working weekend for parents
           In preparing for the weekend, follow same
           instructions as for first parental project.

Discussion Time

Since this project is to discuss the need for revising
(or refusing to revise) parental standards it is assumed
that the parents will have a definite standard upon
which they have mutually agreed. In discussing the
possibility of revising parental standards apply the
following question to the standard upon which you are
mutually agreed:

"When should we amend or rescind this statement?"
Answer by one of the following:
1. Never. It is too basic to our sense of right and
    wrong.
2. When Johnny is 16, old enough to drive and to
    assume some responsibility.
3. If Johnny is still living at home after he is of age.
Apply this question to every statement or guideline
which makes up your standard for the home.

Work Time

Do a quick final check on your mutual standard. On
the basis of your discussion concerning revisions, you
should now have a standard which may be divided into
three basic categories:
A. We can foresee no circumstance which would

cause us to change our opinion on this. Our children will adhere to it.

B. We cannot foresee that we would change our opinion, but we will allow Johnny to make his own decision at age _____.

C. This represents the chosen lifestyle of our home. Even adult offspring living at home must adhere to this.

As you attempt to revise standards, make sure that you are clear on the difference between controlling the lifestyle of the home and controlling your child for life.

Additional reading suggestion: The book, *For Women Only,* Tyndale House, edited by Evelyn R. and J. Allan Petersen, has an excellent chapter for parents dealing with standards. It is titled, "Mrs. Billy Graham Answers Your Questions" by Linda Raney and Joan Gage.

PART FOUR
The Parents Face a Casualty

6
Emergency Procedures for Coping With the Immediate Crisis

If the roof suddenly fell in and destroyed your home, how long would you stand amidst the rubble asking, "Why did this happen?" before you began to ask, "What am I going to do?" Often I have seen pictures of families standing in the ruins of their home which has been destroyed by some catastrophe. Invariably these people, while still in an obvious state of shock, are picking through the debris trying to salvage something of what remains.

Where to begin is a big question because there is

nothing orderly about a house with the roof fallen in. Not only are contents damaged or destroyed, but everything is shoved around in the crash. Hopeless as it may appear, one thing is certain. Before reconstruction can begin, the debris must be sorted out, discarded, salvaged or hauled away. It is there one must begin. One piece or one load at a time.

How very similar to the scene which a parent confronts immediately after a crisis which threatens to disintegrate the family. When our lives cave in because of the actions of a son or daughter, everything seems to be a jumbled, disorderly, chaotic mess. Standing amidst the shambles of our private emotions and our corporate family life, we wonder how we will ever reconstruct anything meaningful.

There is one basic similarity between reconstructing a caved-in life and reconstructing a caved-in house. In either case, the longer one remains in the limbo of "Why did it happen?" the longer the reconstruction process is put off. "What am I going to do about it?" is a far more constructive question.

If you are trying to put your life back together after the rebellion of an offspring, the first area to consider is the people involved. You. Your mate. The children yet at home. The son or daughter responsible. I mention this individual last because once the crisis has come, once that person has made his choice, the focus should change to rebuilding the family life for those who remain. You can no longer put all your time and effort into trying to change the course Johnny is taking, to control him any longer, or to prevent the inevitable mess he is making of his life.

Let's begin with yourself. You may experience one of several emotions. Numbness and detachment. Despair.

Anger. Resentment. Whatever the feeling, its force is likely to be so great that it will be debilitating. Merely functioning will demand great effort on your part. Getting through the necessary daily routine will require determination. At this crucial state, that is a sufficient goal. Get through the day, one hour at a time. This is not a good time to try to find solutions for problems the future is certain to hold. Concentrate on solving the immediate problems of each hour.

At such a time as this, the Christian parent should learn to lean on the Lord Jesus Christ. The temptation is to say, "Lord, if I could just understand, it wouldn't hurt so much!" But the need is to pray, "Lord, I know you promised peace that passeth understanding (Philippians 4:7) and I need that right now."

It is important even while you are still very much in need of comfort that you make an effort to give comfort to those who share your sorrow. Your mate must have some loving attention because each of you suffers and each of you has needs. Obviously you need each other in a very special way when you are facing a common heartache. You must reach out and be sensitive to each other's suffering. Grief can quickly drown you if you think only of yourself.

There are two extremes to be avoided in any suffering. One is trying to be too brave and never allowing yourself to give in to the emotional upheaval you feel. Amy Ross Young has expressed this so well in her book, *By Death or Divorce* in the chapter, "The Burden of Being Brave."[1] Years of pent-up grief will do strange things to people, physically, emotionally, spiritually.

The other extreme to be avoided is that of making a lifelong hobby of your suffering. It is important that, even in the very beginning of your suffering, you shift the focus and force yourself to see that there are others who stand beside you and ache as you ache. You need not mouth a lot of superficial phrases promising rosy tomorrows which you do not foresee, nor do you need to say things you do not yet believe. But do force yourself to see that you are not the only one who is hurting. This will help you give a quiet "I love you" at the right time or a simple, encouraging "We'll make it, honey." It shows that other person that you care.

Special care must be taken to help the children yet in the home. Teenagers are likely to do a tailspin. If Johnny was the oldest and was looked up to by his siblings, those siblings will have special problems. Linda was the younger of two children. She had always compared herself unfavorably to her brother in spite of parental effort to avoid this. She wanted to achieve everything he achieved in life because she felt obligated to do so. He always did everything right, was seldom in trouble at home and never in trouble out of the home. She would at times convince herself that she was almost a second-class citizen because she couldn't live up to this self-imposed goal to be like her brother.

When he was twenty-one, her brother suddenly decided he wanted a completely different lifestyle. He packed a small suitcase and left his wife, telling her not to bother to look for him, that he was going to San Francisco and when he was ready to see anyone from the family he would let them know. There was an angry scene in which the parents tried to reason with him but to no avail.

"For once I'm going to do what I want to do," he said and off he went. It was just before the holidays and the entire family felt as if they had been torn apart. But Linda was hit especially hard. Suddenly her model disappeared. This brother whom she had felt so obligated to emulate was no longer worth emulating.

Linda was angry. She was even panic-stricken. She made a lot of irreversible decisions during that period of her life because she felt, "If my brother couldn't make it, what chance do I have?" She broke off a serious relationship with her boyfriend and for the first time experimented with alcohol. She was still a minor. She went out one night to a friend's home and got drunk. While her parents tightened up their supervision and were very firm about what they expected from her, they also tried to find ways to help her through the difficult period. They especially tried to find ways to show her that she was important to them as a person. They realized that she was going through a very confusing time trying to sort out her feelings.

Finding ways to help is important at this stage. At any given moment one family member will be experiencing more difficulty than the others. This is not to say that it will be easy for anyone. But because emotions tend to fluctuate, the one having the most difficulty will vary from day to day. That person needs the encouragement of everyone in the family at that time.

I recall a period of extreme difficulty in our own family during which we were all having a hard time coping. One day my husband was finding it especially hard just getting from one moment to the next. One of our daughters just sat down beside him for a few minutes. With a gentle nudge in the ribs she said very quietly, "Oh, Dad, it will be okay." That was all he needed to get him through the day.

One very practical way to aid everyone in getting through the "debris" period is to go out as a family for a meal. At home there is nothing to keep you from giving in to your emotions 24 hours a day. But if you go out for a meal or to some public function where you normally expect to maintain control over your emotions, you will be forced to call a moratorium on your problem for a few hours. While those hours spent together may not be altogether joyous, they will provide a much needed diversion.

One of the most difficult problems parents face in the initial crisis is the relationship with the rebelling child. Johnny will not be thinking rationally; therefore, it will be difficult, if not impossible, to predict his reactions to anything you say or do.

Robert had given his parents an especially hard time. At nineteen he declared his right to leave home, took an apartment with his girlfriend and made it very clear he wanted no interference from his family. Certainly he didn't want them to try to locate him, although he was remaining in the same city. Yet within a week he had informed his sixteen-year-old brother that his parents obviously cared nothing for him because they had made no effort to see him at the service station where he worked.

Any contact made in a situation like this may be interpreted as interference. Yet no contact at all may be interpreted as a lack of love. The rebelling son or daughter will even begin to blame the family because the new relationship with the family makes him feel like a stranger.

In Robert's case, as he began to feel left out, he poured out his feelings to one of his peers. The friend happened to be the son of old family friends. Having heard only one side of the story this family soon contacted Robert's parents to intercede for him.

"He feels you will not let him come home," they said. "Can't you reconsider and let him come back?"

Of course the well-meaning friends were quite surprised to learn that Robert and not his parents had demanded the new relationship which had left him feeling so alone.

"Leave me alone" uttered by a rebellious child in the hysterical beginnings of a full-scale rebellion must be taken with reservation. What the child is really wanting at that stage of his life is the best of two worlds, yours and his. To him that makes sense even if his parents know it is unreasonable, irrational and impossible.

A parent must move cautiously at this point. Don't try a lengthy lecture on irrational behavior. He will not comprehend it at this point anyway. On the other hand, don't give in to every whim Johnny has. You will be reduced to a puppet on a string if you attempt to do everything he seems to be telling you to do. Remember that now that he has made the break and precipitated a whole spectrum of family problems, you must think of yourself, your mate and your other children first. That means you will weigh every decision by how it will affect the rest of the family.

To begin with, you must see boundary lines clearly. All major decisions will fall into two categories: "I may not approve, but it's your life, Johnny," and, "You may not like it but it is our home, Johnny." The life that Johnny is bent on messing up for years to come is his to mess up. But that home which he persists in destroying in the process is your home to protect. If that means taking a hard line with Johnny, so be it.

Robert's parents came to two decisions soon after his break with the family. If Robert wanted to shack up with a girl at his own expense, it was his life. But if they did not want him to bring her home for a meal or for a weekend, it was their home. There was no need to allow things to go on in their home of which they did not approve.

This is a principle about which we have always been firm in our home. I believe it is something which parents must begin to practice when children are very small if they expect to enforce it when a teenage crisis comes. For example, when our girls were small they knew that the children who came to play had to play by the rules of the house. When their friends jumped on the beds I always informed them, "Our girls are not allowed to do that, so as long as you are playing in their home, you cannot do it either."

There are many people who have a hard time making decisions of this nature but it is an important principle for anyone who values his home as his own. I believe it affects many areas of your life and the more you stick by that principle the easier it is to apply it in time of crisis.

As a small girl I observed how my parents entertained and how they visited. Through their example I learned that there are certain manners to be observed by the host and hostess and there are certain manners to be observed by the guests in the home.

Over the years we have entertained all manner of guests in our home. Most of them I enjoyed immensely. But I remember one who came whom I did not enjoy. He was a stranger to us but was traveling with one of our good friends. In that capacity he was a dinner guest in our home. In a short while he began talking on a very controversial subject and spent the next several hours in an argumentative mood. As his hostess I was greatly offended, not by his views which he certainly had a right to have, but over the manner in which he conducted himself as a guest in my home. Needless to say, he was never invited back.

I still believe that one's home should be one's castle. No one, not even Johnny, should be allowed to force you to endure things in your home against your wishes. An estranged child seldom conducts himself as a family member. Neither does he behave as a guest. How does one handle an adult offspring who does not conduct himself properly in his parents' home?

Joe related to us how he handled the problem. His son had married very young, against his parents' wishes and advice. He was so angered that his parents would not give their wholehearted approval that he refused to see them for over two years. Finally, after the birth of the first grandchild the young couple visited the parents. It was a terrible week for all of them. The daughter-in-law was sloppy, lazy and thoughtless. She barely took care of the baby. Observing none of the social rules for guests in a home, the couple took advantage of a complete vacation with sister and mother providing the maid service.

After the week was over, Joe called his son aside. "How you live your life is your business," he said, "but I will not tolerate unthoughtful conduct in our home. Until you can come back and expect to assume your share of keeping things picked up and conduct yourself as something besides a freeloader, you will not be welcome."

A question many parents face is how to make social contact with their children, especially those involved in sexual misconduct. Robert's parents handled their situation in a manner with which they were comfortable. After a brief cooling off period they felt it was time to make some contact with their son. They did not wish to have him and his roommate come to their home, and even if Robert and his roommate had invited them to visit at their apartment, the parents did not wish to do that, either.

Instead, they chose a way in which they could have some time with Robert without appearing to condone his actions. They contacted him at work, arranged to take him to lunch and spent an hour with him eating and talking of everything except the issue which had driven them apart. After several such contacts, Robert began dropping by alone to visit his parents. Of course the relationship could hardly be expected to be the same. When conversation is guarded in order to avoid infringing on one another's rights, the relationship remains quite superficial. But it is the best one can hope for, for the time being.

Learning to cope is an essential part of being a parent. Watching people who have suffered and who have learned to cope with sorrow gives a parent courage when most needed. One of our friends from seminary days has seen more sorrow than anyone of our acquaintance. When we first met, we had a year-old daughter. He and his wife had already lost one child and his wife was pregnant again. Since that time he has lost another child, his wife, his mother and a sister. A singularly successful pastor and a much sought-after speaker, he seldom refers to his sufferings. He refuses to allow himself to dwell on that side of life because to do so would tap the energy he needs. However on one occasion we were visiting after a space of many years and inevitably some of the incidents from the past surfaced.

At the close of the visit I made a passing comment concerning our heartache over a daughter who was estranged at the time. Instantly our friend was all sympathy. To him sorrow is sorrow. Whether through death or other circumstances the loss of a child causes a great deal of suffering for a parent. It is because parents have no control over suffering that it becomes necessary to cope.

I have another friend whose ability to cope is an example worth mentioning. When her son was three years old he was found to be epileptic. Through the years he became progressively worse. When he was about ten years of age, I recall visiting with them and my friend explained that, while the seizures could now be completely controlled, the medication was a problem. He was constantly under heavy sedation. There were other problems also. They encountered some rather ugly facts of life along the way. At least one move was precipitated by a neighborhood which was not receptive to the afflicted son.

Early in her son's illness, my friend realized that a parent could react in one of two ways. She could stand among the debris of broken dreams and bitterly denounce God, fate, and the inadequacy of medical science, or she could find a way to cope. She decided to cope. She became involved in educating the public on epilepsy. She was appointed by the governor of her state to serve on a committee which deals with problems of epilepsy and other handicaps. Nothing she did could diminish her son's illness. But it heightened her ability to cope. So effective was that ability that I forgot that behind her beautiful, spontaneous smile my friend still suffered a great deal.

One week before his twentieth birthday, her son died in a home accident related to a seizure. We lived over 300 miles away and it was some time before I learned of his death. When I did I called her. We talked briefly, then she said, "I know he is happy now. I know where he is and I know that no one is laughing at him any more."

In that moment I realized to what extent she had suffered as a mother, even while she coped. I was so moved I had to hang up. I couldn't talk anymore. Her hurt was there for 17 years. But she coped and her life was better for it. Many others benefited because she learned a constructive way to cope.

Life is never quite the same after a severe emotional trauma, but it does go on. We cannot wait for the hurt to go away before we begin to meet life again. We cannot waste emotional energy wishing things were different. Coping can only begin when we face the situation for what it is: there is a problem which cannot be solved to our complete satisfaction. But life does go on and for those willing to make the effort it can be infinitely worth living.

7
Eight Do's and Don'ts for the Post-Crisis Period

1. Do show optimism for the future.

You don't have to show optimism for Johnny's future, although it is hoped that in time that will come. But you must show optimism for the home, the siblings who remain and the family's future. Dr. Martin Symonds, a psychiatrist specializing in adolescents, has this to say concerning optimism.

"Parents have to be optimists. They have to have faith in the world and its future, or they can't expect their children to have it. Without faith, it's like an Army captain muttering, 'We'll never take that hill,' before the battle begins. If you really feel that the world is in a hopeless mess, hide it. Whatever you say should be honest, but don't confuse honesty with total confession; not everything must be said. Don't share your uncertainties about the future with your adolescent. Allow him to explore the future on his own, with your support."[1]

Perhaps at no time do adolescents need the optimism of the parent more than when an older sibling has plunged the family into chaos. And as Dr. Symonds pointed out, it should be an honest optimism without false pretenses but also without total confession. Your personal fears concerning Johnny's future should be kept to yourself.

2. Do "double" efforts to rebuild a normal life for the rest of the family.

If siblings convey a need to discuss Johnny's problem, discuss it. But take care to get the discussion off dead center as soon as possible. Let the home life revolve around something else. Plan a weekend trip for the family. Make plans for a summer vacation. Spend an evening playing some family games.

Mother, bake someone's favorite dessert each day. Even if there is little interest in food, the family will take the cue from you and enter into the effort to regain a degree of normality. Father, how long since you have taken the family for a treat at the local ice-cream parlor or root beer stand? Don't wait for an urge; at this stage the only urge will be to quit. Think of something the family would enjoy under normal circumstances, then do it.

Have you been neglecting the world of your other

children? Do you know what is going on at their school these days? Is art, music or sports important to them? Show an interest in what they are doing. It is essential that they know you care about what interests them.

Johnny's problem will be with you for a long time, but at least with concentrated effort you can force it to the side. The life of the home need no longer revolve around it.

3. *Do communicate your love for Johnny to his siblings.*

The children left at home need assurance that the parents still love Johnny. It is characteristic of the adolescent to react negatively to whatever the parent says or does. He easily misinterprets parental words and actions. He sees implications which are not intended. In the post-crisis period, siblings will be going through a confusion uniquely their own. Initially they may be very critical of what Johnny has done. But they may quickly become defensive if the parent appears to communicate a lack of love for Johnny.

No doubt this sibling feels personally threatened when he senses "Johnny has done something wrong so now my parents do not love him." Certainly he will sense his own capacity to do "something wrong" and thus jeopardize parental love for him. Defending Johnny will to a certain extent constitute self-defense. It goes without saying that parents should not criticize or judge Johnny to other children in the home. Siblings feel pulled in between, even when parents are not consciously critical of the rebelling child. Once the actual crisis is over they are apt to feel a sibling sense of loyalty which dictates that they must defend each other.

In some cases one of the siblings yet at home may

develop a sympathetic relationship with Johnny which will lead to further division in the family. This will bring about a series of problems. "Should I allow this child to visit Johnny? Should I discourage the relationship."

To actively and vocally discourage the relationship will probably accomplish the exact opposite, so the parent in this situation is wise to move cautiously. As to visits, it will of course depend on a number of facts. How old is the sibling? What kind of trouble is Johnny involved in? Certainly a minor should not be allowed to visit Johnny if he is involved in drugs or other activities with legal implications. If, on the other hand, the remaining sibling is approaching adulthood and if Johnny's problem does not have legal implications the parent may find it the better part of wisdom to allow a visit. Some older adolescents make very objective decisions about what they see if they are not feeling pressured to take sides.

4. Don't feel you have to explain or apologize for Johnny's actions to friends and relatives.

The social contacts of the entire family may suffer some long-range effects from Johnny's actions. Some friends of long standing will communicate their feeling that you are to blame for Johnny's problems. You may find it desirable to cool certain relationships because friends cannot handle your situation. Parents do not need to continue relationships which pressure them to explain or apologize for what their adult children do.

In the case of the extended family, you may have to handle unpleasant situations differently. For out-of-town close relatives there may come a time when you must tell most of the details. You should not feel pressured to do this until the immediate crisis is over. Then choose a time when you can either write or telephone in privacy and give the essential facts which you feel the family should know. This is your decision. For those who have praying relatives, it gives great comfort to know that someone is joining with you in interceding for Johnny and upholding you and your mate as well.

5. *Do be realistic about personal consequences of Johnny's actions.*

While the thrust of this book may be taken to be the absolving of parents from blame, in no way do I imply that a lack of guilt guarantees a lack of consequences. Parents cannot escape the continuing effects brought about by Johnny's rebellion. For every family with the problem of a rebelling offspring there will be a set of consequences which must be borne corporately. Contrary to the past decade of "do your own thing" philosophy, it is impossible for anyone to do his own thing without affecting another person. Just as it is important for parents to see that they are not necessarily failures because of the course of action Johnny has taken, so it is important for parents to face realistically the tangible problems brought about by that action.

There are times when parents will find it absolutely necessary or essentially wise to relocate. Roots may be deep but moving may become necessary. Is that fair? Perhaps not, but seldom is life fair. In some cases a parent's job may actually be jeopardized by the actions of an offspring. These are big decisions and should be made with proper consideration, counsel and prayer.

6. *Do face the financial crisis wisely.*

Serious financial problems often result from a crisis

with an offspring. The problems can become especially complicated when there are siblings yet at home who are looking to college or who have other needs. Big decisions may be involved.

Once Johnny has made his break, the parent should first ask himself the question, "Can we afford to help him?" If it would present a financial problem, then except in the most extenuating circumstances, the parent should offer no assistance whatever. If on the other hand the parent can easily help Johnny, the question then becomes, "Is it good for Johnny to have parental assistance at this point in his life?" Will parental assistance diminish the chance of his living with his own decisions? So long as Johnny has the best of two worlds he will find it very difficult (and completely unnecessary) to be objective about the implications of his decisions.

There are times when a genuine need is there (health, transportation for work, etc.) and the parent is able by some means to meet that need. The ideal, I believe, is to do so with stipulations. An informal contract calling for terms of repayment, some possession held as collateral, anything to help Johnny see that he has now entered the adult world of business where no one gets anything for nothing.

Unfortunately some rather ugly facts of life may present themselves in the financial problem category. Many parents have had to face the unpleasant fact that an offspring involved in drugs soon loses all scruples in his effort to support his lifestyle. Needs quickly overcome former values until the child will take anything of value from his own home to turn into ready cash. Facing reality in this case means taking every possible measure to prevent Johnny's entering the home when no one is there.

I recall that in one place we lived the parents of a girl

who had become involved in drugs came to us with a unique problem. An heirloom ring of considerable value had been handed down to the daughter. By rights the ring was hers. But the parents felt that in a larger sense it belonged to the family and that all measures should be taken to preserve it for that reason.

Fearing the daughter would sell the ring for drug money, they brought it to us requesting that we keep it in our safe. This we did for some time. As her parents had feared, there came a time when she demanded the ring but they assured her it was in safekeeping for the future. The story has a happy ending for this girl later left the drug scene, went back to college and became a successful journalist. The ring has long since been returned to her and she treasures it as highly as did her parents.

7. Don't neglect your health.

Many parents of rebelling teens are in the prime age bracket for illnesses of a stress nature. They also age very rapidly when forced to go through several years of trying to solve all the problems heaped upon them through the rebellion. If you need proof of this statement just compare before and after photographs of parents in this category.

One father was accused of giving a ten-year-old photo to a newspaper which was recognizing one of his recent achievements. Friends saw the picture and teased him about trying to appear younger. His best friend was aware of some of the problems this father had recently encountered but even he was surprised to discover that the picture was only two years old. The father had been through problems which produced those aging worry lines.

It is essential that the parent concentrate on breaking stress patterns induced by the offspring's behavior. Certainly the annual physical, or semiannual one, becomes of prime importance. The parent must do everything possible to establish a positive mental outlook. I have heard parents testify to the fact that with God's help they were able to establish this, even when they didn't know the exact whereabouts of their son for months at a time.

8. Do seek out a sympathetic listener.

Beware of those listeners who, even while expressing sympathy, are all too eager to point out your errors: "You should have done this." "I wouldn't put up with that." "Why don't you make Johnny do this?" Some of this well-meant but ill-timed advice will be forced upon you, but you should avoid soliciting it. It can only complicate the picture and it will certainly not increase your ability to cope.

At this stage it is good for the parents to communicate with others who have known the same trials. Perhaps the parent will even feel the need to seek counsel in order to sort out his feelings. Such counsel must be sought with care. One father seeking the counsel of an older professional shared some of the burdens he was facing with his children. Unbelievably, he came away with nothing but the counselor's account of his own highly successful adult children. Hopefully such incidents are rare, but I cannot tell you to seek counsel and guarantee that the first counsel you receive will be helpful. You may come away as did this father, more discouraged than ever.

But this is part of life also. You must sift through advice which is handed out unthinkingly, without feeling or proper understanding. Some of it may be worthless. But don't give up. Keep trying. One day there will be just the right person who will say, "Do you need a couple of waterproof shoulder pads? Come on over."

One mother who has faced problems with several of her children related how she and her husband were once facing a crisis and approached a trusted older friend. He told them, "I don't know what I can do, but I can listen." And he did. Today that mother is doing the same for others. She doesn't claim to have any answers but she is a good sympathetic listener and she is saturated in the Word of God which is her chief source of encouragement.

We began this chapter by saying that a parent should be optimistic for the sake of siblings. I close by submitting that the parent should be optimistic for himself also. Many times those offspring who put parents through years of pain somehow survive those turbulent years and do a turnabout. As Christian parents we must cling to the promise that the training we have given them as children will in the end be the training to which they will return. Hope for the future is something we must never lose sight of as we pray daily for those children who stray.

PART FIVE
The Parents' Right to Life

8
Is There Life
After Johnny?

After the immediate crisis is past, after long-range adjustments are made, after new relationships are spelled out there remains yet one more problem for Johnny's parents: "Where do we go from here?"

How do parents face the future? Can emotions so traumatized by the crisis ever be healed? How can parents put their own lives back together again? Many parents are defeated at this juncture because they fail to deal with that last nagging question—Can there be life after Johnny?

Right or wrong, many parents build all of life's plans around their children from the moment of conception. Those parents invest as much as a quarter of a century in the lives of their children. If Johnny manages to spare his parents the pain of rebellion, if he manages to respond to their investment in a manner which pleases them, upon his departure there is only a small matter of empty rooms to deal with. But if, on the other hand, after those 25 or so years the parents are left with little or no relationship with Johnny because of problems of rebellion, there is a very large matter of empty lives with which to deal.

Any latent creativity concerning plans for the future, the fifties or the retirement years have remained undeveloped because the parents have assumed that Johnny will always be around to brighten their lives. Now that he is no longer around, the parents must call upon some resources which have lain quite dormant for a number of years. They must begin thinking about a future which possibly does not include Johnny.

Dreams of extended family relationships, vacations with grandchildren, reunions and all that makes for continuous enjoyment of offspring must now be laid aside. With all illusions gone, parents must now find new ways to make life worth living. The parents' primary goal must now be to reconstruct their own personal lives.

The parent must decide for life

The parent who discovers life after Johnny must act decisively. His first step is to choose life over mere existence. The parent must recognize that there is a difference between coping and living. As essential as it is to learn to cope, this must never become an end in itself. Coping is not the same as living.

Unfortunately many times when the crisis is past the parent who has learned to cope mistakenly assumes that he has done all that can be done. He mistakes the ability to ward off hurt for the ability to find solutions. There are those who build walls to avoid further pain and become so used to the walls that they are unaware of their presence. This is known as a withdrawal process and it happens to the best of people.

Parents of estranged children are certainly vulnerable to emotional withdrawal. In the course of my husband's ministry he often administers a personality profile test to those with whom he counsels. He has found this particular test to be an extremely valuable tool. It is neither complicated nor extensive enough to threaten the average person. The purpose of it is to show a picture of the individual as he views himself. One of the problems it pinpoints is that of withdrawal.

Recently he had an interesting experience with this process. A father was taking a repeat test after a span of four years. This man who is normally outgoing and very sociable had gradually become quieter, keeping to himself for the most part. Since his work demands constant contact with people there were those who had become aware of the change. The man himself was completely oblivious to it. He was greatly surprised when he found the results of the test to show that he had become very withdrawn since the previous testing.

In pinpointing the events of his life in the intervening period it was discovered that his first testing had been administered just one month prior to the onset of a great crisis with his teenage son. In the four-year period, the crisis had been somewhat resolved and the father had learned to successfully cope with a great many unpleasant situations. But that was as far as he went.

In dealing with his own hurt he had subconsciously cut himself off from all but the most rudimentary social contact. He went through the motions on his job but he actually lost interest in people and in life. He was existing. In this man's case, once he saw the pattern he had created, he was able to break it by concentrated effort. It demanded decisive action on his part. His success was due largely to the fact that he was not satisfied with mere existence. He chose for life.

The parent must assume control of his own situation

A parent can assume control of his own situation even if he cannot control Johnny. In fact, when a parent assumes control of his own situation it has nothing to do with what Johnny does or does not do. It has to do with the parent's reactions, his outlook and his personal plans. It has to do with assuming control of self, not of offspring or of circumstances.

When our children were quite small we had a beautiful water spaniel puppy. For reasons long forgotten we neglected to have the necessary shots for him and when he was about eight months old he contracted distemper. For days the girls kept vigil over that sick little dog. Our middle daughter still remembers how unfeeling her father was when he found her kneeling beside the dog with dishtowel half in the dog's bed and half on the floor. The sight of it provoked some rather stern words from Father. Our daughter felt it was completely inhuman to scold her simply because she could not concentrate on such mundane chores as drying dishes when Rags was at death's door.

When the dog died the girls cried for two days and no amount of comfort would stem their tears. On the third morning our youngest, then six years old, marched into the living room and made an announcement. "Well, I've had enough," she exclaimed. "I'm not going to cry anymore!"

And that was that. She could not change the circumstances but in her childish wisdom she took charge of her own situation when she decided not to cry anymore.

It should be noted that taking charge of one's situation is a very individual matter. Our daughter did not wait for her older sisters to make the first move or even to agree with her. Hopefully both parents will come to the place where they will opt for living over mere existing. But to wait for one's spouse may defeat the one trying to assume control of his situation. Someone must make the first move. It must be made whether or not the spouse falls into step.

Follow decision with action

My husband's secretary once tacked a cartoon upon the office door. It was a picture of five frogs sitting on a log and there was a caption which asked the question, "If there were five frogs on a log and one decided to jump, how many would be left on the log?" A fold in the cartoon formed a pocket from which the curious could draw the card containing the answer. It read, "Five would be left. Deciding to jump is not the same as jumping." The parent who is truly decisive will follow decision with action.

Finding life after Johnny is a self-help program which demands determination over feelings and action over inertia. It calls for a schedule which allows for development of the physical, mental and social areas of life. The parent doesn't have to launch a full-scale self-improvement program. But he should take inventory of the neglected areas of his life and take immediate steps to correct the situation.

Consider first the physical. In addition to health which was discussed in chapter seven, the physical area of life involves such things as exercise and personal grooming. What type of exercise have you enjoyed in the past? Have you neglected it during the period of Johnny's rebellion? Has the tennis racquet been confined to the closet for the duration of the disaster? Is the fishing pole gathering dust? Have you forgotten where you put your bowling ball? Now is the time to drag out those things and put them to use.

Perhaps you have always wanted to learn a certain sport. Now is the time to add this to your schedule. Recently my husband became interested in sailing. One reason he enjoys it so much is that he finds he must give it his complete attention. It is a total diversion from work or problems.

Be realistic about your ability and your physical fitness and choose something at which you can expect a degree of success. You don't need one more thing in your life to undermine your self-confidence. And of course it is always essential that any exercise program be undertaken wisely.

Our personal physician has consistently advised us against jogging because he is quite sure we will not keep up with it. At our age he believes that strenuous exercise should either be done regularly or not at all. For us the doctor's advice has consistently been, "Take a brisk two-mile walk every day."

A good evaluation of personal grooming would be in order at this point. In the face of great emotional trauma over which the parent has no control, he can easily lose interest in lesser matters over which he could exercise control. It is a fact that when we lose interest in life, we sometimes lose interest in personal appearance. Examine this carefully. Determine to give a certain amount of time each day to personal appearance. Include such things as manicures, pedicures, skin treatment, hair care and all those extra areas which may need attention.

How about your wardrobe? Have you let it go just because you were in such a zombie state you could not decide what to buy? Or you neglected it because you didn't care about such trivial things in light of the greater problem?

In addition to the physical, take inventory of the mental area of your life. Stretching the mind seems to be a necessary thing for people who have reached a plateau in their lives and are floundering around not knowing what to do next. Have you contemplated taking classes at the local college? Although I am not creative I have noticed that for those who are, there are numerous opportunities today. Most local colleges offer many classes designed to encourage adults to develop their creative skills. Macrame, pottery, stained-glass design are but a few of the many classes available.

For the more academically oriented there are also correspondence courses. I discovered that the local extension service from one of our state universities offers a correspondence course in German. Because I had been interested in learning it and have some personal background with the language, I enrolled. In my experience I have found few things which occupy the mind more completely than the study of a foreign language.

Certainly you need not be limited to local colleges or correspondence courses. Set up your own reading program in a subject you wish to study. Attend some lectures. The opportunities are there for the parent who decides to stretch his mind a bit.

Last of all let us consider the area of social contact. The social area of life is extremely important for that parent who is electing for new life after Johnny. It is not something which will come automatically. The parent must determine to get out and make contacts. Don't wait for the mood to hit. Many people can very easily absorb themselves in work, problems and projects and never be aware of missing social contact.

Sometimes I do this myself. But in the process I become rather introverted. Usually when I break the routine and get out it is not because I suddenly decide, "Hey, I want to get out of this house and see someone," or "Wait, honey, I'll pack a bag and go with you this trip." It is usually because I force myself to break the pattern, get out, communicate with someone. Just visiting an old friend or going somewhere different is enough. Whenever I return from the experience of communicating with some other human in any small way, I am again a different person. More responsive. Happier. More content. More objective about my problems. The point? If you wait to resume social contact until you feel the need you will never change the pattern. In reconstructing a life I am convinced of one thing, actions come first and feeling follows.

It should not be assumed that every parent needs the same amount or the same type of social contact. Neither should it be assumed that you will have the same needs after your traumatic experience. It may be that through your experience you have had to drop contact with some casual acquaintances. People are sometimes insensitive. Friends may need you to fulfill their needs but show little compassion or concern for your own needs.

It is difficult to maintain much social contact with those who either have not understood your problem or who have not been able to handle it. Still you need some social contact. The circle may be smaller, more intimate. It may be made up primarily of new friends met in the post-Johnny period. Build your own circle and cultivate friendships carefully.

Another form of social contact is social action. This is a very constructive way to deal with your own needs while meeting another's. Volunteers are needed in so many areas. Your political party, the local hospital, your church, all of these agencies are in constant need of people who are willing to get involved. Perhaps you have learned something through your experience which awakened an interest in a certain area. In the beginning of the traumatic experience a parent may wish to get as far away as possible from anything which reminds him of the problem. But after time has done its work many parents feel differently. They want to get involved in preventing some of the things which caused them so much heartache.

Recently a mother who has faced problems with all three of her children remarked that she would like to work in some capacity with troubled teens. At this point she doesn't know how or where but she is determined to prepare herself for the opportunity should it come.

There are no set rules for developing the physical, mental and social areas of life. Each parent has different needs, different likes and dislikes. The important thing is to actively pursue those things which are a personal challenge. At this point in life the parent must consider his own needs. If the parent is to find healing for his damaged emotions, if he is to reconstruct a meaningful life, he must consider his personal needs.

The parent who continues to consider Johnny's needs

to the exclusion of his own will impede the emotional healing process. There must come a point where the parent acknowledges, "Johnny has made his choice. I can no longer concentrate all my efforts toward preventing him from destroying himself. I must now see that I am not destroyed in the aftermath."

Emotional healing can never be contingent on a change in Johnny. That may never happen. The parent must not wait for Johnny to change before he begins to reconstruct his own life.

Ultimately, reconstructing the life will involve reconstructing the marriage and for some, reconstructing one's spiritual life. These subjects will be dealt with in the next two chapters.

If every parent had a success story this book would not be necessary. But so long as the propagation of the human race continues there will be parents who will face disappointment and depression effected by the actions of their offspring. If the reader can be helped to discover that there can be life after Johnny, the objective of this book will be met.

PARENTAL PROJECT
Assuming Control of Self

Project: For the individual parent

I. *Think* about these things
   Assuming control of your life demands some positive thinking, a habit which you may have lost through the crisis with Johnny. Use the following exercise to get you started again. Timing yourself for one minute, complete question #1 with as many answers as possible. Repeat with question #2.

   (1) I think these things make life worth living—

   (2) I really enjoy—

II. *Ponder* these questions
   a. I would feel better about myself if
   b. I would like the way I look if only
   c. I feel good about the way I look when
   d. My wardrobe definitely needs
   e. My skin needs some attention   __(yes) __(no)
   f. My hair needs some attention   __(yes) __(no)
   g. My weight needs some attention   __(yes) __(no)
   h. I need a checkup   __(yes) __(no)
   i. Do I get enough regular exercise? __(yes) __(no)

III. Projects for getting your mind off your problems
   1. On the basis of the above questions, compile a list of shopping needs. Decide whether ques-

tions e-f need professional appointments.
Make them
2. Squander a full afternoon on personal grooming
3. Read an Erma Bombeck book
4. Take a friend to lunch
5. Spend an afternoon at the park
6. Investigate local opportunities for mind
stretching (college classes, seminars, crafts,
hobbies)
7. Learn a new skill
8. Attend a concert
9. Investigate needs for volunteers in your
church, your community and your political
party
10. Do something nice for your spouse

9
Can We Begin Again, Lord?

For the Christian parent, if there is to be life after Johnny it may be necessary to begin again in a spiritual sense. We are never the same after a traumatic experience. For better or for worse we are changed through those things which touch our lives. The trauma experienced through the loss of an offspring to some form of rebellion may cause a temporary regression of the spiritual life. For this parent, the most important question becomes, "Can we begin again, Lord?"

When I first met Gordon he was making a new beginning in his spiritual life. As a Christian he had spent years shoving aside unresolved problems. The resulting accumulation of guilt made serious inroads into his relationship with God. Then one night someone told him what to do about his guilt, real or imagined. That night Gordon made a new beginning. This is his story.

Although Gordon is a warm, loving and outgoing individual who holds a responsible position in his community, for years he saw himself only as a parent who had failed. He went through a divorce when his children were approaching adolescence. There had been problems in the marriage. In a sense, the divorce simply exchanged one set of problems for another. In the first place, as a Christian Gordon did not really believe in divorce. Death of a marriage meant death of an ideal and ideals die hard. He felt very guilty over the marriage breakup.

In the second place, he felt extremely guilty over the effects (real or imagined) of the divorce upon his sons. Much of this guilt stemmed from one past incident which he could not forget. He remembered a day when his tenderhearted little son was moved to tears because the parents of his best friend divorced. The boy was so affected by this that Gordon took his son in his arms, comforted him and promised, "Son, you don't ever have to worry about anything like that happening to your parents. It never will." But of course it did. And the thought of that broken promise haunted Gordon for years.

Because Gordon is both intelligent and aggressive, he had no problem finding success and wealth. But he was a lonely man. There were nights, he confesses, that in his loneliness he cried throughout the night for his boys. Inevitably he slipped into the pattern of trying to buy their love. Elaborate vacations were standard procedure for the times they were with him. To illustrate the extremity of his problem, Gordon tells how he spent enormous amounts of money decorating his bachelor apartment, buying sterling silverware, table linens, etc., for a holiday visit from his sons. He wanted everything to be perfect for the little time they would be together.

Such unwise parental actions generated a predictable response from two growing boys. Gordon was first used by his sons and, in time, actually rejected. When he woke up to the situation, he made a series of readjustments in his dealing with them. In time he developed a good relationship with his sons, but he still carried his load of guilt.

Meanwhile he remarried and his life began to take on a new dimension. He was no longer plagued by loneliness but he felt responsible for every problem the boys faced in their teenage years. Everytime he heard that one of the boys was in trouble, he blamed himself. "I wasn't there when they needed me," he explains.

The boys were grown before Gordon faced the regression in his own spiritual life which had been caused by unresolved guilt. It happened one night at a seminar sponsored by Campus Crusade. There the speaker instructed those attending to write down on a piece of paper all mistakes and sins of the past. Then they were led to pray, confessing them to God. Finally they were instructed to write across the list "Forgiven."

"It was a new beginning," Gordon declares. "All of my confusion and guilt, He took care of." From that new beginning the reconstruction of his spiritual life took place.

To begin again you must wipe the slate clean

For those who would make a new beginning spiritually,

the first step is to wipe the slate clean. That means dealing with mistakes. Certainly we as parents do make mistakes. But as one mother observed, "I did the best I could with the knowledge I had at the time. I've asked the Lord to forgive my mistakes and I know He has." First John 1:9 must become a reality in the life of the parent who needs a spiritual new beginning:

> If we confess our sins, he is faithful and
> just to forgive us our sins, and to cleanse
> us from all unrighteousness.

Gordon found forgiveness on this basis, not because someone said, "Stop feeling guilty."

Wiping the slate clean also means dealing with bitterness. There can be no spiritual renewal so long as a parent feels bitter over what has happened. A parent is very vulnerable to bitterness. Basically, many parents are idealists. There is nothing so positive as an idealist whose values have never been tested. But when those ideals have been through the crucible, the idealist will either emerge a stronger person or a bitter, disillusioned person. It is impossible to remain the same after your theories concerning the most important things in life have been confronted with the ultimate test.

For the Christian, the testing of ideals is part of the maturing process. These times of testing should serve to deepen our relationship with God. Consider Job. Satan thought him an untested idealist. In fact Satan told God that anyone can be strong if you put a hedge around him. But God allowed Job to be put through the crucible. His ideals were tested. And he came out stronger.

After he lost everything, his friends became his accusers and his wife said, "Curse God and die." But Job, after careful self-examination, determined it was a time of testing and his relationship with God deepened.

"Though he slay me," he said, "yet will I trust in him." What could have been a bitter experience became a maturing experience. Out of his suffering came the theme which still expresses the hope of every believer, "I know that my Redeemer liveth!"

Consider also David. He is an even greater example for the parent who suffers because of rebelling children. His son Absalom rose up against his own father. It was a dark time for David. He lost the loyalty of his closest friends. His chief counsel defected to Absalom. A troublemaker erroneously reported that Mephibosheth, grandson of Saul, was seizing the opportunity to stake his claim to the throne. Shimei followed David cursing, spitting, throwing stones and showering the king with dirt. Bitterness could be expected. David had selflessly served the very people who hunted him down. But the crucible—even the trauma of Absalom's rebellion—served to bring David closer to God.

Bitterness is like a cancerous growth. It soon dominates the life which it invades. It accomplishes only one thing, the destruction of the life over which it has gained control.

If Johnny's actions have left you bitter, wipe the slate clean. Confess this bitterness to God. That means calling it exactly what God calls it. It means praying a simple prayer, "Lord, I confess I am bitter. Forgive me."

We begin again by understanding the value of suffering

Second Corinthians 1:2-4 describes the God of all comfort by saying that He comforts us in all our troubles so that we may in turn comfort those in any trouble by the same comfort we ourselves have received from God.

Jennifer recently remarked how she is discovering this truth. Since her children are not yet in school she knows little of the parental suffering with which this book is concerned; however, about a year ago she and her husband went through an extremely difficult period. At the time neither knew how they would survive. Today she states that they learned some lessons they would never have learned apart from the suffering they endured. And the most exciting thing to Jennifer now is that she has met a young woman her age who is experiencing the same difficulty. Jennifer has been able to encourage her.

"I couldn't believe it," Jennifer said, "but I was able to encourage her just by assuring her that we have been down that road ourselves." She is learning that suffering is valuable because it enables us to sympathize with others who have the same problems.

Rarely does comfort come from those who have not known suffering. Experience seems to precede empathy in most cases. Ruth Bell Graham expresses this thought:

> They felt good eyes upon them
> and shrank within—undone;
> good parents had good children
> and they—a wandering one.
> The good folk never meant
> to act smug or condemn,
> but having prodigals
> just "wasn't done" with them.
> Remind them gently, Lord,
> how You
> have trouble with Your children
> too.

Ruth Bell Graham, *Sitting By My Laughing Fire,* copyright © 1977, p. 47, used by permission of Word Books, publisher, Waco, Texas 76703.

The value of suffering as a teacher and a refiner has been expressed by many poets, theologians and song-writers. One of my favorites is Audrey Mieir's beautiful song, "Don't Spare Me."

> Forgive me Lord, I've prayed in vain
> That You would spare me grief and pain,
> But now my blinded eyes can see
> These things were best for me.

Don't spare me trouble if it will bring me close
   to Thee.
Don't spare me heartaches; You bore a broken
   heart for me.
Don't spare me loneliness, for I recall
   Gethsemane.
Don't spare me anything that You endured
   for me.
Don't spare me failure if this is what is best
   for me.
Don't spare me sickness if this will make me call
   on Thee.
Don't spare me suffering, for I recall Your agony.
Don't spare me anything that You endured for me.
   But give me strength to follow Thee.

We begin again by making a new commitment to God

To begin again we must commit ourselves to study His Word, to pray and to be available to comfort others who also suffer. The personal Bible study program of the parent becomes essential to progress at this point. My good friend Lillian explains a time of deep trouble by saying, "I was groveling my way through the Psalms." In the Psalms there is such comfort, even for those times when we are at our lowest.

But beyond the comfort there must come a deeper look at the Word and it must be done on a systematic, daily basis. Begin by setting aside a good time. The earlier in your day, the better. Try a book study. Or do a character study. Have you ever read the life of Moses or David, looking at their attitudes and reactions to problems? This makes an enlightening study.

Whatever you choose to study, do try to look beyond the actions recorded and find the attitudes which are revealed by the people involved. Keep a notebook and make note of these attitudes. Write down your observations. Especially note any which seem to parallel your own attitudes at this stage of your life. On a separate page you may want to list any spiritual lessons learned through your experience with Johnny. Also note any negative attitudes which the experience has caused to surface. You will soon begin to see through your study how attitudes affected the outcome of many situations recorded in the Scripture. Personal applications will become obvious. The Word of God can help you grow through this experience.

Add a new dimension to your prayer life. In addition to praying for Johnny and his continuing problem, pray, "Lord, make me a blessing to someone today. And Lord, teach me through thy Word." Make a prayer list. Pray for other parents who suffer. Keep a prayer diary or a file.

Many years ago while attending Biola College I received a prayer file from a friend. A simple recipe size file box, it contained cards indexed for each day of the week plus one section marked "Answered." Through the years it has served as an aid to prayer. When our children were small and demanded my constant attention, there were many times when the cards were propped up above the sink or on the ironing board because time was so short. But parents whose children have grown are more free to arrange a daily encounter with God over a prayer list. Make this a part of your recommitment program.

As you study and pray you will be prepared for that third part of your recommitment program, comforting others by the same comfort you have received in your suffering. Remember as you do that it is enough to say, "I know what you are going through." You don't have to repeat all your trials. That is no comfort unless you are citing some specific point at which the Lord gave special comfort.

What is needed most is a good listener. Sharing a verse or a passage of Scripture is also important if it has been important to you. Preaching a sermon, on the other hand, is not being helpful. Praying *with* the one who suffers as well as *for* him is a comfort.

No matter what the trauma in life, the spiritually oriented person will not be the same in its wake. Suffering over children is the same as any other suffering insofar as the spiritual lesson learned is concerned. Ultimately every individual must face that incident in life which reduces one to the knowledge that there is no human help available. Such times as these teach us a more complete trust in God's dealing with our lives.

Such times also prompt a reassessment of spiritual goals. Emerging on the other side of the traumatic experience, the parent may see that some of his worthy goals were slightly off-course. For example, a mother may have been challenged by the scriptural example of

Hannah who prayed for a son and then presented that son to the Lord. Hannah's story may have inspired the mother to raise her children in such a way as to be pleasing to the Lord. Her spiritual goal becomes the same as Hannah's. She wants to offer her child in some way to the Lord. And so the mother spends her life endeavoring to mold and shape the life of her child. Her daily prayer is, "Lord, you gave me this wonderful gift, this dear little life. In appreciation for this life you lent me, I am molding and shaping it as you would desire."

Then one day the child grows up, exercises his God-given will in quite the opposite direction of his parents' wishes, and the mother finds herself in a lonely and desolate place. Quite empty-handed she stands with nothing to offer the Lord.

Well, not quite empty-handed. She has herself. Perhaps that is what the Lord wanted in the first place. It is here at this point of desolation that the mother must reassess her spiritual goals. She now offers a revised version of that daily prayer, "Lord, I have nothing left to offer you, except myself. But I gladly offer you that."

Can we begin again, Lord?

PARENTAL PROJECT

Spiritual Recommitment

1. If you haven't already done so, set aside a special time for daily Bible *study*.
2. Make a list of spiritual lessons you learned through your experience.
3. Make a list of other parents who are going through similar experiences. Pray daily for them.
4. Count your blessings.
5. Set aside a regular time for prayer.
6. Make a list of parents with success stories. Thank God for the way He has worked in the lives of those sons or daughters and pray for their continued obedience to Him.
7. Attend a retreat.
8. Visit someone who is lonely.
9. Visit a Christian bookstore. Buy a new book. Read it!
10. Count your blessings again.

10
We Still Have
Each Other

When Johnny is the last child to leave home the parents are left with an additional problem. For weeks, months, and sometimes years they have concentrated all their efforts toward finding a solution for Johnny's problem. There has been little time to think of anything else. Now they are faced with the inevitable. Johnny is gone and there is nothing they can do about it. There are no tail-spinning siblings left in the home to demand parental love and attention. With Johnny gone these parents are confronted with an immediate void. For better or for worse they are back to square one. They are alone. But they still have each other. Or do they?

"The teenage years present a real test to the solidity of the marriage." This astute observation was made by my friend Peggy, a high school counselor. We had been discussing some of the problems of adolescents when she shifted the perspective to the problems of parents of adolescents. Of course anything which puts a strain on the home will likely put a strain on the marriage. And vice versa. I think there are only three things about which couples fight: sex, money and children (make that four if there are in-law problems). It depends upon which stage of life they are in as to which item occupies top place on the list. As children reach the teenage years, parents find themselves quarreling more about their offspring.

When a home has been through a teenage rebellion crisis which has culminated with Johnny's leaving home, it is possible that a reassessment of the marriage must take place. If the marriage is in trouble, the situation back at square one becomes, "We still have each other if we work at it."

I do not believe that good marriages result by accident or by Cupid's irresistible bow. Show me a happy couple and I will show you two people who work at their marriage. There are critical periods throughout a marriage where this is especially true. The post-Johnny era is one of them. Parents who seek to find life after Johnny must recognize the need to work at their marriage. Certainly the post-crisis reconstruction process will not be complete so long as the marriage is in trouble.

Put the past behind

Earlier we spoke of the need to wipe the slate clean in

order to begin again spiritually. This is also true when it comes to the marriage. In the post-Johnny period, working at marriage is like beginning all over again. The first step is to determine to wipe the slate clean by putting the past behind. There are two negative principles which are fundamental to putting the past behind. Don't blame each other. Don't look back.

To blame one another for Johnny's problem may be a temptation. But rarely can any family disaster be laid at the feet of one parent. In such cases where it may be justified there must come forgiveness and a frank acknowledgement that you are mates in all of life for better or for worse. So be generous with your spouse. There is nothing so useless as the admonition, "You should have done it this way," when there will never again be the opportunity to do it *any* way.

It is so important that you and your spouse lay aside the past and determine not to look back. We must make decisions every day of our lives. Human error is a necessary risk of daily living. How tormented we become, how unsure of ourselves, how incompetent, if we continually examine those decisions and wonder, "Did I do right?" This is especially true concerning parental responsibilities. No other job compares to parenthood in that by the time we learn to do the job it is too late. Accept the fact that a stage of your life is over. If you can't look back remembering the laughter, don't look back.

Renew your courtship

Once the past is dealt with, parents should apply themselves to today and tomorrow and all the tomorrows they have together. Reconstructing the marriage is to some extent like renewing a courtship. You begin again.

Only now you are older, wiser, perhaps less starry-eyed. You are beginning from a different perspective. Still you begin in much the same way.

What pleases your mate? What are the things you can do for your other half? Think about your courtship period. You wanted to do things to please that person who was always in your thoughts. Cooking a man's favorite dishes, achieving the look he appreciates and saying things he likes to hear are all part of a woman's daily routine during the courting period. The man in turn often surprises the object of his affections with inexpensive little gifts, an impromptu outing, compliments and tender words. Favorite dishes may now be low calorie, compliments may take a different form and outings may necessarily be less strenuous, but the basic principle is just the same.

In his book, *Men in Mid Life Crisis,*[1] Jim Conway writes optimistically concerning parents left alone after the children are gone. "Children also influence marital happiness. In the early years of marriage, children tend to build an emotional bond between a man and his wife. During their adolescent years, children tend to drive down their parents' emotional happiness. After the couple has passed the empty nest and mid-life crisis, marital happiness improves with the absence of children, allowing the couple to relate to each other more intimately." This should be the goal of parents in the post-Johnny era, to relate to one another more intimately.

Encourage one another

In addition to courtship renewal there should be a determined effort to encourage your mate to pursue that which is important to him (her). Is there something you can encourage your mate to do simply because you know he (she) has always wanted to do it? Is there a new hobby which should be started? A neglected one to be resumed? A degree to be pursued? A talent to be developed? Whatever you do to encourage your mate will surely benefit both of you in the long run.

Set new goals

Even if you are not primarily goal-centered as a couple, this is a good time to set a few. It gives new purpose to life. Make your goals in two categories: "Let's share today" and "Let's plan for the future."

Our youngest daughter left home last week. She has returned to the city of her birth to seek employment. The nest seems empty, the house much too quiet and my husband and I are lonely. But we prepared ourselves by setting some goals. That daily walking we always intended to do together is now a definite part of our routine. At six A.M. we take a two-and-a-half mile hike.

There is also a long-range goal involved here. I want to hike to Havasupai village. For those non-westerners I should explain that this last vestige of paradise with its famous Supai falls is located in the floor of the Grand Canyon. More than any other place, this is where I would like to go soon. But I know I must train for such an undertaking. My husband is less enthusiastic ("If you're going with your first husband, you are going to have to hurry up!") or perhaps just more realistic about our physical abilities. But he is willing to pursue the goal with me.

At this point it is too soon to tell if we will ever be in shape to hike the eight miles down to this idyllic spot and then climb back up again, but whether or not we make the long-range goal we at least begin each day with a short one: "Let's share today."

Whether or not you take a daily walk together, you should set aside some portion of the day to do something together. Sitting across the table from one another doesn't count. Years ago a frustrated mother of two toddlers related to me that her doctor told her, "You and your husband have to find something you can do together every day if it's nothing more than going out in the yard and pulling a weed or two." What is necessary for younger parents is just as essential for parents in a post-Johnny period.

Vary the routine

Not only should you set goals which allow for more time spent together, but you should also seek to vary your routine. Routines develop out of necessity but can become very dull over the years. Does your husband like to sneak out late at night to the Dairy Queen, the Pizza Hut or to the Dunkin' Donut shop? For years you couldn't leave little Johnny home alone. Then came the adolescent period. Any time the urge for a late night foray hit hubby, Johnny had the car.

Now there is no excuse. Perhaps your wife has always wanted to eat out more but your responsibilities as a provider for a growing family made it economically impossible. This is a good time to revise the budget to include an occasional night out for the cook. There is no better period in life for varying the routine than right now.

Compromise creatively

During the post-Johnny period, parents may spend

prime time together if they learn to make use of the creative compromise. The day our daughter left, I cried. All day. I cleaned her room, packed away the few things left behind and talked to her poodle who spent the day sniffing out every corner of her room. But the next day I packed my suitcase and went with my husband to a three-day conference.

I had the usual excuses for staying home. I didn't have time to go. I had deadlines to meet. I couldn't spare three more days in addition to my time off for crying. My husband had two reasons why I should go. I needed to get away. He wanted me with him. So we compromised. I packed a briefcase, my manuscript file and my typewriter. I worked at the motel during the day. He attended the meetings. Together we had dinner each evening, attended the evening sessions and went out for late night snacks with friends.

We both accomplished what we set out to accomplish and we spent some prime time together in the process. In fact it worked so well we intend to do it again. With only two schedules to consider, a couple can do much more together if they are willing to compromise a little.

Seek stimulation

As you and your mate work through this adjustment period, concentrate on finding situations and people who stimulate you. Whether through a new challenge or some new friends, aggressively seek the stimulation which adds zest to life.

Begin to set goals for the future. What is it you have always wanted to do but never dared? Now is the time to investigate every possibility. Some ideas may have to be discarded. Let's face it, we can't all climb Mount Everest or become a world champion golfer, but others may be found to be within the realm of possibility. Possible goals may include a new home, remodeling the one you have, taking some night classes together, or traveling.

Have you dreamed of going to Europe? Investigating the possibility may show you it would be easier than you thought. Did you know that, although a first class round-trip ticket from L.A. to London costs $1,972, it is possible to make that trip on the same airline for $387?[2] There are many ways to cut costs if you are willing to put the time and effort into planning your own trip abroad. Even for those who do not have to budget that stringently, a do-it-yourself plan is still a great way to go because planning such a trip is half the fun.

You may not want to travel to Europe, hike to Havasupai or even go out for a midnight pizza. But it is essential that you invest the time and effort required to reconstruct your marriage after Johnny has gone. This investment will pay high dividends because the complexion of your entire future depends on it.

According to Jim Conway, that future could equal half of your married life. "Because families have fewer children, parents today begin to experience the empty nest when the parents are in their forties. Yet since life expectancy has increased dramatically—both parents may expect to live into their seventies—couples now have half of their marriage without children in the home."[3]

In families where the relationships remain good, at least a part of those years will be filled with extended family situations involving grandchildren and married sons and daughters. But many parents no longer consider it necessary to plan their future around the extended family after the children are grown.

"Death of a Fairy Tale"[4] is the story of one young couple who wanted traditional closeby grandparents for their children but whose parents had other ideas. Both sets of parents retired the same year. One moved to California and the other to Florida. It was a shock to the young couple to find that their parents wanted to build a life for themselves in spite of their love for their children and the good relationships they maintained. In time the couple adjusted and came to see that their parents had a right to make such choices.

Parents who lose temporary contact with their adult offspring because of problems of rebellion will feel a great void. For them, making creative choices concerning the future is more than a right. It is essential for survival. I do not advocate all parents relocating in Florida or California (or Arizona!). But I do advocate that parents in the post-Johnny era concentrate on what seems right for the two of them. When parents begin to ask, "What can we do for each other?" and "What can we do together?" it does not mean that they have suddenly grown selfish. It means that they are consciously striving to strengthen their own relationship. In the long run anything which strengthens the parents' marriage will prove beneficial to everyone concerned.

PARENTAL PROJECT

Serious and Silly Things to Do With Your Spouse or For Your Spouse

Project: For the couple

1. If you are the cook in the family, plan a special meal just for your spouse.
2. Plan an evening out for your spouse. (A date, in other words!)
3. Set aside an evening at home to talk about wild dreams for the future. (It costs nothing to dream, so always begin with the dream and then see what can be fit into the budget and the physical limitations.)
4. Encourage your spouse in some specific area today.
5. Plan a weekend away in the near future. (Together that is!)
6. Buy a gift for your spouse today. (It doesn't have to be expensive, just thoughtful.)
7. Invite some friends in for dessert. (Don't talk about kids!)
8. Pick up some travel folders today and study them together.
9. Spend an evening browsing through your favorite department store looking at home furnishings, clothing or hobby items.

10. Encourage your spouse to talk about him-(her)self this evening. Ask him (her) to tell you something "funny about myself" or "something I've always wanted to do." (Be a good listener!)
11. Go out for a midnight snack.
12. Have you hugged your spouse today?

PART SIX
The Parents' Gift of Love

"If" for Parents

If you can love your child,
   through each stormy teenage year
If you can keep your standards
   when his begin to disappear
If you can dream for your child
   and watch the dream begin to crumble,
If you can reason with him
   when you're tempted to berate
If you can remember his laughter
   long after he begins to grumble
If you can pray and hope and
   not go blaming fate
If you can bear to hear the counsel you've given
   twisted by a rash and angry son
   or watch him go his way until he's broken
Then stoop to pick him up, no matter what he's done,
If you can wait and not be tired by waiting
If you can separate the lying from the one who lies
   and seeing the hate, love the one who does the hating
   yet not seem cold, unfeeling and pompously wise
If you can love when he no longer needs you
If you can reach out when he seems to turn away
If you can live with optimism too
   by looking beyond the present to a future day
If you can dream and wait and love and pray
   then you can learn to smile along the way.
   What's more, you can truthfully say
      "I did my best,
      now let God take care of the rest."

11
Love Letters to Sons and Daughters

When a parent faces the myriad problems of an estranged child he often finds himself in a position where he can offer that child nothing but love. The parent cannot offer support for fear of condoning his child's actions. He cannot offer guidance for fear of interfering. He cannot offer financial aid for fear of underwriting a lifestyle which he abhors. He cannot even smooth over some of the rough places for the child because to do so would diminish the child's ability to live with his decision. Through this period the parent is faced with the rather complicated task of communicating "I love you, Johnny" without communicating "I approve of what you are doing." When the parent takes the necessary pains to express his love, he is doing the most important thing he can do for his child.

There will be a never-ending problem of communication. Although Johnny has demanded freedom from parental authority he is very unsure about how that freedom is supposed to affect the relationship with his parents. He knows he doesn't want them to tell him what to do. He is relieved when he realizes they have faced the facts, recognized that he is an adult, and discontinued their nagging. But often he is not prepared to face the other changes which follow.

Telephone conversations will be guarded, letters rather stilted, and the entire relationship will be somewhat superficial during the initial period of the estrangement. Parents can understand the cause of this but usually Johnny can't. Perhaps he has a sense of guilt which interferes with his objectivity. Perhaps it's just that his parents are much older and have more experience and a better perspective. They realize that relinquishing authority also means being relieved of responsibility. There is a vague sense of relief about this for some parents. A certain alleviation of pressure comes with the end of a war, even when all the battles have been lost.

Unexpectedly, Johnny may find himself bewildered by the whole process. He may begin to sense that his parents are somewhat relieved and he sees this as an indication that they are glad to be free of him. (He had expected it to be the other way around.) He may express his confusion by accusing his parents of not loving him, of being distant, of favoring siblings yet at home, or of discouraging a mutually intimate relationship.

Understandably, complicated communication problems develop. Explosive conversations constitute only one part of the problem. If the estranged child moves to another city a whole new set of communication problems develop. Sometimes the child drops out of sight for months at a time. Sometimes he gives a false address, using a friend's home for a mail drop. Keeping in touch is always a possible problem. Even when Johnny writes regularly, the parents may have a very difficult time communicating because they know Johnny is constantly trying to read between the lines. Every word may be suspect.

In this chapter are some excerpts of letters written by parents to estranged children. Each of these parents was attempting to assure the child, "We love you." But each tried to do this without compromising his own values or diminishing the responsibility of the estranged child. This is no easy task.

The letters are not presented as perfect examples or as final solutions. They were chosen because they represent a variety of problems: a widowed mother counsels her daughter concerning some of the consequences of cohabitation outside of marriage; a father explains to a son in prison why no one has complete freedom to live as he chooses; a mother sympathizes with a daughter's suffering; a father deals with a son's imagined rejection; and a mother reaches out to a son whose contacts are becoming fewer and farther between. Hopefully the reader will gain from these letters some insight into handling communication with estranged sons and daughters. The letters are, in a very real sense, love letters from parents to sons and daughters.

Letter #1

A widowed mother shares this correspondence with her

daughter. The occasion of the letters was the fiftieth anniversary celebration for the paternal grandparents. The daughter writes:

Mom,

Today I received an invitation from Aunt Trish for the 50th anniversary party for Grandma and Grandad. She enclosed a note saying how they were all counting on my being there since I am the only granddaughter, etc., etc.

Have you told them about me and Joe? I am afraid Grandma and Grandad might not understand and I certainly don't want to be accused of ruining the whole day. If they don't already know and it came out at the party they might be hurt. I wouldn't want everyone in the family upset with me for spoiling their party.

Could you explain that I just couldn't make it?

Judy

The mother replies:

My dear daughter,

Your letter concerning the party for your grandparents came yesterday. I have thought a lot about it and have decided that the time has come to try to communicate about some of those things left unsaid when you made your bid for "freedom." Three months ago when you and Joe decided to set up housekeeping I did everything I could to prevent your doing so. But I was forced to accept the fact that you are 21. I have tried to live with this fact even though your actions go against everything I believe in and everything I stand for. So far my decision to accept the facts has worked to your advantage. Now you will see that this will not always be the case.

To answer your two questions: No, I have not told your grandparents (or anyone else) that when you moved 300 miles away it was to move in with your boyfriend. And no, I will not make any excuses or explanations for you. I know the invitation calls for R.S.V.P. You may go or not go as you wish, but it is your responsibility to make your own excuses.

When you were little and sometimes misbehaved at your grandmother's home it was my responsibility to correct and to control you. Sometimes it was even necessary for me to apologize for your actions. But when I relinquished the right to control your actions I was relieved of the necessity of explaining them.

I am sorry if this sounds hard, but that is what is meant by living with your decisions. Remember when you went away you said, "I am of age and I don't need your permission to live with Joe," and I said, "Judy, this is a big decision. Are you sure you can live with the consequences?" You immediately answered, "What consequences? It's nobody's business." For three months living with your decision has simply meant living with a man with whom you think you are in love. It has meant having no mother to answer to, no one to tell you what to do or to act as your conscience.

But deciding what to do about family relationships is one of the consequences of your decision. You will have to live with that—and handle it.

You are right of course when you say that your grandparents will be very hurt. When two people celebrate a 50th anniversary as your grandparents are soon to do, it is because they long ago made an important decision. They committed themselves to one another. That gave love a chance to grow, to withstand the hard times and to survive for 50 years. You are right to think that people who have experienced this will have a hard time understanding what you call love.

You say that you love Joe and that you want to spend this part of your life with him even though neither of you is willing to legally commit yourself to one another for the rest of your lives. Judy, without commitment you do not have love. You have a relationship—and a very fragile one at that. You know nothing of the real love experienced by two individuals who are willing to commit themselves to one another.

Without commitment there is no incentive to work at a relationship. In fact the absence of commitment is contrary to the whole idea of developing a relationship. Without commitment there is no development, only questions: Is he the right one? Will I find someone I love more? Can I hold on to him? Do I dare make plans for next year? How long will it last?

When you commit yourself to someone you enter the relationship knowing, "We are in this for better or for worse. It is to our advantage to work at it to make it the very best." On such decisions 50-year marriages are built.

Now my dear one, if you will think about these things and if you will handle the anniversary party problem yourself, I promise that I will consider the subject off limits in future letters. I love you.

Mom

Letter #2

A mother finds herself in the common position of having to watch a daughter suffer through a rocky romance. The mother has never approved of the relationship and has counseled seriously with the daughter on why it was not a good one. Still she loves her daughter and feels deeply for her during a painful period.

By means of a simple greeting card the mother conveys this message:

When you hurt,
I hurt.

Letter #3

A son has followed the narcotic trail to prison. While he had been aware of the possible consequences of his involvement he had thought that he could gamble and win. From prison he wrote his father that he had learned the hard way that his actions led to inevitable consequences. He could not, however, come to terms with the fact that his younger brothers were having such a hard time in school because of what he had done. The father responds (in part):

. . . It is interesting that you should say what you did about freedom—"Why can't we ever really be free to live our own life without having to worry about hurting those close to us?"

I am sure you are referring to your brothers who are having such a bad time of it. Perhaps I can best answer your question by sharing with you an ancient Jewish story. It seems there were several men out in a rowboat. One man, lost in thought, was carving away with his knife on the bottom of the boat. Suddenly one of the other men looked up and cried, "Stop that! You're cutting a hole in the bottom of the boat." And the fellow with the knife replied, "Leave me alone, I'm cutting this hole under my own seat."

Sometimes when young people say, "I have the right to live the way I please," it translates, "I have the right to do what I please no matter who it hurts." This is a serious abuse of freedom and anyone who lives like that will soon find himself very much alone. . . .

Letter #4

This couple found that, although their son wanted to proceed with his own life apart from the family, he could not accept the fact that they were rebuilding their own lives apart from him. He accused them of being angry with him, of rejecting him and of cutting him off.

The father tries to explain:

Son,

I am sorry that you feel that we are angry with you. I'm afraid that you really don't understand our feelings at all. What you did has not made us angry. It has not made us want to strike out at you. It broke our hearts and crushed our will to live. It brought your brother home from school because he could not carry on under the circumstances.

When you love someone it is entirely possible to recognize his right to live his own life but still be utterly crushed by what he is doing. For a time all of us were absolutely incapable of functioning as a family at home. But we have come to realize that we must change that.

We never meant to convey that we were cutting you off. We will always love you, son, and something has gone out of our lives which no one can replace, but we must consider your brother at this point also. We have to pick up the pieces, pull together and rebuild our own lives. We hope that you understand.

Always,
Dad

Letter #5

These Christian parents have watched their son slip farther and farther away from the family as he enters a lifestyle contrary to their sense of values. The immediate problem is that the son no longer keeps regular contact with his parents.

The mother expresses their concern:

Dear son,

We are praying this will reach you. It has been so long since we have heard from you. Please, won't you try to keep in touch? No matter what your perception of our relationship is, we do love you very much. You might not feel that this is true because we have refused to help you financially. But I'm sure you realize that we simply cannot contribute to the lifestyle you have chosen at this time. To just bum around with all that word implies, to dabble on the fringes of the drug scene, and above all to waste your excellent mind and many talents is, to us, unbelievable. It is hard for us to bear, impossible for us to support.

While on the one hand we want you to succeed

with your rock group, on the other hand we feel sure that you are not going to find happiness in that direction, even if you find success and fame.

I feel compelled to remind you that the Scripture says there is pleasure in sin for a season. If you are still reading—I'll add that as a child of God, you will never find true peace or contentment while living in rebellion against Him. And besides, I hope you will think sometimes about how much God loves you. It is a great comfort to us to know that God loves you even more than we do. His love is not dependent upon good behavior and He knows all about your problems, your attitudes, why you have chosen your present course and what it will take to turn you back to Him.

Now I promise, no more preaching. I'll just say we all miss you very, very much. Please do write us and let us know where you are and what you're doing. It is such a big world to lose a son in.

Lots of love,
Mom and Dad

12
"The Greatest
of These . . ."

To say that parental love takes many forms is to express nothing new. It has been said many times and in a variety of ways that a parent's love is not always verbalized but is often communicated in other ways. For example, parents discipline because they love. That's why the spanking is preceded by the lecture, "This hurts me worse than it does you." A child can't possibly believe that, because he has no comprehension of the amount of pain involved when a loving parent is forced to mete out discipline.

My father is a no-nonsense person. He used firm disciplinary measures but he never appeared to me to be stern or unfeeling. Now that I look back, I can imagine that some of the discipline he handed out must have been very painful for him.

Once he allowed my brother to spend the night in jail when he could easily have secured his release. (That was the last night my brother ever spent in jail. In fact, he grew up to become a minister.)

Ron was about sixteen when the incident took place. He was working for a man who owned a filling station. The man thought the sun rose and set in Ron because he had proved himself to be such a willing and able worker. One of the fringe benefits of the job was the occasional opportunity to drive the boss's pickup.

One evening Ron and a friend were passing by the station and, seeing the truck, they decided to take a ride. The station was closed and the boss had gone home. The two boys climbed into the truck and drove off. (How can you ask permission if no one is around?) Very shortly, someone notified the station owner that his pickup was gone, and he called the police and before you could say "juvenile delinquent," the boys were in the city jail.

My brother's boss was mortified. He refused to press charges. "Had I known it was Ron, it would have been okay. He can use that truck any time he wants to." But the police refused to release my brother except into my father's custody. The owner called my dad and begged him to go get Ron. My mother dissolved into tears and I watched the whole procedure realizing only that a crisis of great importance had confronted my parents.

In the midst of all that confusion my father made his decision. "Let him spend the night in jail," he said. "He had no business taking that truck without permission."

Only after I became a parent did I appreciate how hard it must have been for my father to make that decision.

In the course of this book we have discussed some rather drastic decisions which a parent must face. "This is our home, Johnny, and you will not be allowed to destroy it." "It is your life, Johnny, and if you insist upon messing it up, we cannot stop you." When spoken out of parental love such decisions cause a great deal of pain. It would cause no pain to turn your back on Johnny if you did not love him. There is a great deal of pain involved when you love Johnny and you are forced to make decisions "for his good."

As the parents' love passes through the crucible of Johnny's rebellion, the parents must cling to the hope that someday Johnny will understand. Only in retrospect do children comprehend what their parents try to communicate through discipline: "I am doing this because I love you."

To fully comprehend parental love, one must experience it from the giving end. My brother is the firstborn in our family. I am next in line. When we were both in high school he coerced our parents into allowing him to join the Navy. When he left, my mother cried. All day. And all night. And the next day. And the next night. She cried so much that my father threatened to call the recruiting office to see if they ever inducted mothers.

Frankly, I couldn't understand her problem. I thought that the Navy was a very convenient place for my brother to be at that stage of my life. It was not until many years later when my husband and I took our firstborn off to college that I even began to comprehend the void which my mother had felt when Ron left.

Parental love is something which is taken for granted by children who experience it. The only children who are acutely conscious of something called parental love are those who are denied it. My husband once counseled a young man who grew up in an affluent family from the upper social register in an Eastern state.

By his own definition, this young man lived a typical poor little rich boy existence. As a child he was conscious of the fact that he had everything except his parents' time and the love it represented. I, on the other hand, grew up taking for granted that my parents loved me. I gave it little thought because I assumed everyone had it. When I went to college I began to see that there were many young people who had vastly different home situations. Only then did I consciously verbalize what I had always accepted: "My parents love me."

Remembering how I took my own parents for granted helped me survive some of those experiences I faced as a mother of teens. As our girls were entering the teenage years I took pen in hand one day and with tongue in cheek penned these words:

"As a mother of girls who have reached their teen years I sometimes find myself examining their actions and words for the barest hint that I am loved or at least needed. But teenagers express such things only in books. Parents of teenagers are seldom loved and almost never appreciated. At best they are tolerated and our only encouragement may come in the signs that our teens are mostly more tolerant than their peers."

I wrote it in a rather tolerant mood of my own, but as time went on it became more difficult to be philosophical about the teenage attitude toward parents. The memory of my own attitude toward my parents sustained me many times. As a teenager I went through the critical phase, the impudent phase, the condescending phase. With each phase I am sure that I must have made it painfully clear that I considered my parents totally inadequate for their job. I doubted many things about them during those phases of the teenage uglies. But somehow it never occurred to me to doubt their love.

If parents did not love, they would not cry. Parental heartache is vividly described by one father who wrote of seeing his son destroy himself on heroin before he was old enough to vote. Recalling one scene with a psychiatrist, the father stated that the doctor turned to the mother and demanded, "Why are you crying? That kind of emotional reaction is not going to help." And the father commented on this scene, "Her firstborn shooting himself full of heroin and the doctor asked, 'Why are you crying?' "[1]

There is but one answer for those who would stem the flow of parental tears altogether: do away with parenthood. Earlier in this book I referred to a young woman who opted for non-parenthood because of the risk involved. She asked herself, "Am I emotionally equipped to face the risk of losing a child through teenage rebellion?" Another young woman of my acquaintance asked herself the question, "Could I have a child and not abuse him?" (She had been an abused child.) In each case these women came up with the same answer. The only way to avoid the risk is to avoid parenthood altogether.

Certainly there is an unknown quantity involved in giving life to a child. There is no clause on the birth certificate warning the parents, "This model will self-destruct in fifteen years or less. To avoid injury to parent, do not attach too closely." Parental love is a risk. In fact, love is a risk.

Love is a risk because it involves a relationship. There are many things in life which we may prefer to do with another person but which we can do just as well alone.

We can live alone, eat alone, work alone, travel alone. The accomplishment of the task does not demand a relationship. But we cannot love alone. If we love there is at least one other person involved. Love demands a relationship.

With every relationship there is the potential for sorrow as well as for joy. This is more evident in a parent-child relationship because it is more permanent. Other relationships are often discontinued when something goes wrong. Yesterday I read the case history of a woman who discontinued a friendship with another woman because she felt it was not a good relationship. They had widely differing personal goals which impeded the natural progress of the friendship. So it was set aside. Discontinued. End of relationship. End of problem.

With a parent-child relationship it cannot be so. This is not a relationship which is set aside simply because the tears have begun to outweigh the laughter. When it becomes obvious that parent and child have widely different personal goals and the result is a deteriorating relationship, the parent does not simply quit loving the child and put an end to the relationship. It is because we continue to love that we must sometimes continue to cry.

If a gift may be defined as something which costs the giver, then parental love may quite accurately be defined as a gift. I have come to see that the love of my parents is the most valuable gift they ever gave to me.

When we own something of value, it is normal to take precautions to preserve it. Our home is furnished primarily with furniture which was once best described as "family attic." With the passing of time some of the cast offs have been reclassified as American antique.

One of our favorite pieces is an oak secretary complete with round glass door. It once belonged to my mother-in-law. She protected the glass door from numerous little hands over the years and preserved it intact. At the time she decided that she had no more use for it, it was worth at most about $65. We have continued to preserve the cabinet by protecting the glass from misplaced furniture, careless movers or uncontrolled little hands. Because we did not allow our children to destroy it, one day we expect to pass it on to one of them.

Parental love is a thing of great value. Great pain should be taken to preserve it. You may lose the battle to preserve Johnny's morals. You may stand helplessly by as he ruins his health. Your hands may be tied as he jeopardizes his future. You may even lose his love for you. But you must not lose your love for him.

Parents do not normally think in terms of preserving their love for their children. Instead they spend a great deal of time and emotional energy trying to preserve Johnny's love for them. They become frustrated, disillusioned and even bitter because it seems to be a losing battle. Of far greater importance is the preservation of their love for their child.

If I could give just one word of advice to parents faced with the heartbreak of rebellion it would be this—do not allow your child to so abuse your love that he destroys it. If he destroys your love for him, you will both have lost something of inestimable value.

When our middle daughter was living at home just prior to her marriage she had the delightful habit of leaving quotations, which she had typed on little pieces of paper, on my mirror or my bulletin board. One such quotation (source unknown) reads, "We are most of us very lonely in this world; you who have any who love you, cling to them and thank God." Parents of estranged children must hope for the future—that one day Johnny will realize the truth of this quotation. When that day comes, may he still be able to number his parents among those who love him.

Your love for Johnny will be preserved if you take charge of your life, your home, your future. These are not selfish measures. The parent who has the courage to take whatever action necessary to control these things will at the same time preserve something of great value. Finding life after Johnny will, in the end, allow the parents to go on loving Johnny.

There is a biblical passage which has been memorized again and again because of its description of love. Known as the Love Chapter it is found in I Corinthians 13, and has been the basis for innumerable paraphrases. I offer yet one more. This is my personal version of parental love based on I Corinthians 13.

A Mother's Paraphrase of I Corinthians 13

If I speak in the vernacular of my teens and understand the language of their peers, but do not give them love, I am just like so much noise falling on their ears.

If I could tell my children exactly what their future holds, if I knew everything ahead of them, and if I believed that someday each one of them would make it, but did not give them love, I am nothing.

If I give them everything they want, if I sacrifice all I have—even my life—for them, and give not love, they gain nothing.

Parental love is patient even with erring offspring. It is kind to the daughter who is hurting. It never says, "I told you so." Parental love is not rude to the impudent son nor easily angered by his ways. Parental love does not delight in father's dire predictions which have come to pass, but rejoices at the slightest positive sign in the child who strays. Parental love protects the toddler, firmly guides the adolescent, hopes for those who falter and perseveres year after year.

Parental love should never fail. Our plans for the future may fail. Our advice may be stilled. Our knowledge may fall short. For we do not know everything and we cannot control everyone. But we can love.

When I was a young mother, I was a visionary. I had all the answers and knew all the formulas for successful child-rearing. But when my children were grown I put those immature ideas behind me. Now I have no answers, I know so little and my understanding is limited. Only in Heaven can I know the rest. There my understanding shall be complete, my joy will be full and my tears will be wiped away.

Three things I have now—faith that my children will remember their training, hope that this will influence their future, and love that continues no matter what. And the greatest of these is love.

Some tears go with the territory. Love is a risk and love costs the giver something. But love is the greatest gift a parent can give.

Postscript . . .

For my daughters—
I have sometimes not understood you
and I have often disagreed with you
but I have always loved you.

Notes

4. Politics, Peers and Parental Pressures

1. Will Durant, *Caesar and Christ,* (New York: Simon and Schuster, 1944), p. 531
2. II Corinthians 6:17
3. "What's Happening to the American Family?", *Better Homes and Gardens,* May, 1973, p. 2

5. Perpetuating Parental Values in the Home

1. "Healthy Criticism: Crossing the Age Barrier and Communicating with your Children," *Today's Health,* August, 1973, p. 72

6. Emergency Procedures for Coping with the Immediate Crisis

1. Amy Ross Young, *By Death or Divorce* (Denver: Accent Books, 1976) p. 30-36.

7. Eight Do's and Don'ts for the Post-Crisis Period

1. "How to Survive Your Adolescent," *Reader's Digest,* March, 1973, (an interview with Symonds, by Joan Rattner Heilman), p. 106

10. We Still Have Each Other

1. Jim Conway, *Men in Mid Life Crisis,* (Elgin, IL: David C. Cook, 1978) p. 184
2. TWA Timetable, 1979, p. 6,7
3. Conway, p. 180
4. "Death of a Fairy Tale," *Home Life,* September, 1978, p. 45 (Kathryn Haveisen)

12. "The Greatest of These . . ."

1. "What Did I Do Wrong?", *Today's Health,* August, 1973, p. 41